W9-BXG-368

A HANDBOOK
OF DICTION
FOR SINGERS

Italian, German, French

DAVID ADAMS

College-Conservatory of Music
University of Cincinnati

New York   Oxford
OXFORD UNIVERSITY PRESS
1999

FRANKLIN TOWNSHIP PUBLIC LIBRARY
485 DeMOTT LANE
SOMERSET, NJ 08873
732-873-8700

Oxford University Press

Oxford   New York
Athens   Auckland   Bangkok   Bogotá   Buenos Aires   Calcutta
Cape Town   Chennai   Dar es Salaam   Delhi   Florence   Hong Kong   Istanbul
Karachi   Kuala Lumpur   Madrid   Melbourne   Mexico City   Mumbai
Nairobi   Paris   São Paulo   Singapore   Taipei   Tokyo   Toronto   Warsaw

and associated companies in
Berlin   Ibadan

Copyright © 1999 by Oxford University Press

Published by Oxford University Press, Inc.
198 Madison Avenue, New York, New York 10016
http://www.oup-usa.org

Oxford is a registered trademark of Oxford University Press

All rights reserved. No part of this publication may be reproduced,
stored in a retrieval system, or transmitted, in any form or by any means,
electronic, mechanical, photocopying, recording, or otherwise,
without the prior permission of Oxford University Press.

Library of Congress Cataloging-in-Publication Data

Adams, David, 1950–
    A handbook of diction for singers : Italian, German, French /
David Adams.
        p. cm.
    Includes bibliographical references (p. ****) and index.
    ISBN-13 978-0-19-512077-6
    ISBN 0-19-512077-9 (pbk.)
    1. Singing—Diction. 2. Italian language—Pronunciation.
3. French language—Pronunciation. 4. German language—
Pronunciation. I. Title.
MT883.A23   1999   98–12204
783′ .043—dc21   CIP
                                                    MN

            9
Printed in the United States of America
on acid-free paper

FRANKLIN TOWNSHIP PUBLIC LIBRARY
485 De MOTT LANE
SOMERSET, NJ 08873
732-873-8700

Dedicated to the memory
of Italo Tajo

CONTENTS

German / 67

French / 115

PREFACE

This textbook is intended for voice students taking classes in the diction of the Italian, German, and French languages. It is written for the student whose native language is American English. It is also intended for voice teachers, vocal coaches, conductors, and anyone else who deals with the singing of these languages. It can, of course, be used for self-study and reference.

The distinctive aural qualities of any language can be gleaned only imperfectly from a book. It is crucial that students of singing hear Italian, German, and French sung by a variety of native singers. It is likewise important for them to experience the inflections of the spoken languages to the extent possible, and to gain at least some expertise in speaking them. Further, students need to study the grammar of each language as thoroughly as possible. Fluency is not required, but the development of an ear for the cadences, modulations, and phrasings of a language will make a significant difference in the authority with which it is sung.

The study of "diction" can encompass at least three levels:

Beginning: Mastering the basic rules of pronunciation, what sounds result from what letters in what contexts, such as when *s* is voiced or unvoiced

Intermediate: The above, plus mastery of those characteristics of a language that are different from one's native language, such as purity of vowel sounds uncolored by English diphthongs, nonaspiration of consonants in Italian and French, and relative length of sounds (single and double consonants in Italian, vowels in any language), to name a few of the more important examples

Advanced: All of the above, plus a subtle understanding of stress and inflection over longer phrase groupings

This book is ultimately aimed toward helping the student achieve an intermediate level of proficiency, as would be expected in a graduate level diction course. It can also be used for a beginning class, if used selectively. Achieving an advanced level usually requires that the student spend a prolonged period in the country where the language is spoken and practice speaking it extensively. Nevertheless, it is hoped that some of the fine points presented in this book will at least make the student more sensitive to various nuances of language. Taken together, such nuances comprise a potentially powerful expressive arsenal for the singer.

Since "diction" is a word that often has negative connotations (classroom exercises, etc) it might better be called "skill with a language." Having inadequate language skills is equivalent to having inadequate intonation; the music just does not sound right. The sensitive listener will be put off by one just as much as the other, no matter how beautiful the voice.

The International Phonetic Alphabet

The International Phonetic Alphabet (IPA) is an indispensable tool in any discussion of the sounds of a language. Learning IPA symbols is not difficult, at least within the scope of diction texts such as this one. The student unfamiliar with them can learn them as they are presented.

While there is general consistency in the usage of the major IPA symbols among the texts and dictionaries that employ them, there are a number of small discrepancies and inconsistencies. An example is the treatment of German diphthongs: the word **euch** is found transcribed [ɔIç], [ɔyç], or [ɔøç] depending on the book. Glides, also called semiconsonants, are represented in different ways, so that the Italian word **guerra** can be transcribed [gwɛrra], [gŭɛrra], or [gu̯ɛrra].

Such inconsistencies from one book to another are ultimately unimportant, as long as the symbols used within a given book are consistent and clear in what they represent. This book will explain its choice of IPA symbols when necessary. It will also present alternatives commonly found in other books.

Valuable as the IPA is, it is limited in the amount of information it can convey. This is particularly true of inflections over longer phrases. It also must be remembered that the IPA is a means to an end and not an end in itself. It is not uncommon to hear a singer who enunciates all sounds according to the "rules" and yet sounds stilted and unidiomatic. One needs to get past the IPA to the language itself.

[ɑ] and [a]

Until recently it has been customary to represent the sound of the Italian vowel-letter *a* as [ɑ]. This symbol is also used by Siebs for the sound of the German vowel-letter *a*. In French, however, it has been customary to represent the bright sound of the vowel-letter *a* as [a] and the darker version (as in **bas**) as [ɑ]. Since the Italian and German sounds are equivalent to the bright sound in French, it is logical to use the same symbol [a] for all three languages, and to reserve the symbol [ɑ] for the dark French version of this vowel. A number of recent books have adopted this format (e.g., Duden for German, Castiglione for Italian) and this book also does so.

Some books use both symbols for German to differentiate length: [ɑ] is long; [a] is short. This text prefers to use one symbol ([a]), adding the colon [:] when it is long, as Duden does.

Some may object to using [a] in all instances for singing, arguing that this vowel sound is not "round" enough. This enters the realm of vowel modification (see below), an important consideration for all singers and voice teachers. This text prefers to make its points in reference to the spoken language, occasionally discussing modifications for singing, but always assuming reasonable and necessary adjustments for singing depending on context.

Symbols for r: [ɾ], [r], [ř], [rr]

The symbol [ɾ] represents a single flip of the tongue for the pronunciation of the letter *r*. It is commonly used in diction texts for Italian intervocalic single *r*, though not all of them use it. Standard diction texts do not generally use [ɾ] for other languages, however. This results in some inconsistency from language to language, since for the purposes of singing, intervocalic *r* is one flip of the tongue in all three languages: **caro, herauf, j'irai.**

The proper IPA symbol for *r* executed with a roll of the tongue is [ř]; however, for some reason standard diction texts for singers do not use this symbol. For Italian double *rr*, which requires the roll, the symbol [rr] is used. In Italian, the symbol [r] is used when the letter *r* is adjacent to another consonant, and when it begins or ends a word. The reason is differentiation of intervocalic *r*, which should only be one flip of the tongue, from *r* in a consonant cluster, when it may be rolled or flipped. This text will use [ɾ], [r], and [rr] for Italian.

French and German use the conventional symbol [r] for virtually all situations, assuming the flipped sound (except when German uses [ɐ], q.v.). Some texts use [rr] for French in those few situations when a rolled, lengthened *r* sound is called for, and this text will follow that example. The uvular pronunciation of *r* (IPA symbol [ʀ]) is used extensively in speech for German and French, but not in singing.

The Symbol [:]

The colon placed after another IPA symbol is the universally accepted means to indicate that the sound represented by the preceding symbol is to be lengthened. It may be used for consonants, but it is more commonly used for vowels. Thus, the two German words **Stadt** and **Staat** are differentiated in sound only by the relative length of the vowel sound. The sound of the vowel in **Staat** [ʃtaːt] is approximately twice as long as that in **Stadt** [ʃtat].

A problem arises with this symbol in IPA renderings of groups of words or phrases. While the examples cited above would not change, a word such as the Italian **mia** could change. This word is probably best transcribed [miːa] to show that the sound [i] is longer than the sound [a]. The same word, however, is rather different in the phrase **mia madre** (normal inflection) because the stress of the phrase goes to the long vowel of **madre** and the duration of the [i] in **mia** is reduced. Perhaps for this reason many texts dispense with the use of [:] altogether. This book will use [:] for long vowel sounds, since it is a useful visual reminder of duration, which is so crucial to the idiomatic sound color of any language. Use of this symbol will be modified in IPA renderings of phrases to reflect syntactical changes of duration.

For the purposes of singing, length of vowel sound is largely determined by the musical setting. Nevertheless, an understanding of relative duration of sounds as they occur in speech is crucial to virtually all kinds of singing.

Vowel Modification and the IPA

Every voice teacher and reasonably experienced singer is familiar with the need to modify vowel sounds in different parts of the voice. This was referred to above under [a] and [ɑ]. The needs are different for different voice types. Many books with IPA transcription for singers attempt to address this issue by altering IPA vowel symbols standard for speaking to different ones for singing. A few such instances are universally accepted, such as French **les** having [e] when spoken but [ɛ] when sung. Most such changes, however, run into the problem that a given modification works for one voice or voice type, but in another sounds exaggerated or affected. The aim of any vowel modification is to give the illusion of the required vowel sound while keeping the sound beautiful.

Just as a page of music is nothing more than a blueprint for ultimate performance, which can differ from one performer to the next, so IPA transcription is a blueprint, a skeleton, for the singer's realization of language. It is best to use the IPA for singing as it is used for speech. The teacher and intelligent singer will understand that adjustments must be made, but it is not for an artificially imposed IPA symbol to dictate an adjustment.

There is a certain amount of repetition and redundancy built into this text. The basic reason is that repetition will drive a point home, but there is also a cross-referencing purpose. If one wants to check on the vowel sound in the first syllable of the French word **dessein**, for example, it will be found under *closed e* because initial *dess-* results in closed [e] in French, but the same information will be found under *open e* as an exception to the usual pattern of *e* before a double consonant resulting in open [ɛ].

It is assumed that the teacher will supplement this text with materials of his or her own devising, such as homework of IPA transcriptions of complete aria or song texts, readings of texts in class, and listening to recorded examples.

Acknowledgments

The author wishes to thank the University of Cincinnati for granting him the sabbatical leave that made the writing of this book possible. Thanks also to Professor Kenneth Griffiths, esteemed colleague, accompanist, and linguist, for reading the manuscript and providing many valuable suggestions; and to Professor Lorenzo Malfatti for his peerless expertise in matters Italian. Finally, thanks to the many students who have given me the experience over the years that resulted in this book.

ITALIAN

Introduction

Italian is widely assumed to be an easy language to sing, the easiest of all the foreign languages. This assumption may derive from the fact that beginning voice students usually sing in Italian as their first foreign language; thus, if beginners sing Italian, it must be easy. While Italian is grammatically easier than German, and is much more phonetic than French (and English), it is difficult to speak and sing Italian well. Indeed, singers who have perfected French and German are often surprisingly unskilled in Italian.

Every language has distinctive sound characteristics that result in its own unique color. Italian has always been justly praised for the purity of its vowel sounds. Just as important to the overall sound color of Italian, however, is how it treats consonants.

For achievement of an intermediate level of proficiency with Italian diction, the following points need to be mastered on a consistent basis:

1. Purity of vowels, with particular attention to unstressed syllables
2. No diphthong in pronouncing [e], [ɛ], [o], and [ɔ]
3. Appropriate "lift" or brightness to [a] and [ɛ]
4. Long sustained vowels in stressed syllables before a single consonant
5. Proper linking of vowels between words
6. Basic understanding of open and closed *e* and *o*
7. Short single consonants
8. Long double consonants
9. Forward articulation and nonaspiration of consonant sounds
10. Relative lengthening of *l*, *m*, *n*, and *r* when initial in consonant clusters

1

International Phonetic Alphabet (IPA) Symbols for Italian

Vowels

[a] **amo, fama**
[e] **vedo, stella**
[ɛ] **bene, bella**
[i] **mio, addiritura**
[o] **colore, dottore**
[ɔ] **sposa, memoria, povero**
[u] **tuo, crudele, fortuna**

Fricative Consonants

[v] [vv] **evviva**
[f] [ff] **farfalla, buffo**
[ʃ] [ʃʃ] **scendo, lascia, pesce**
[s] [ss] **sasso, stesso**
[z] **rosa, smania**

Lateral Consonants

[l] [ll] **libro, giallo**
[ʎ] [ʎʎ] **gli, figlio**

Affricate Consonants

[tʃ] [ttʃ] **cerco, caccia**
[dʒ] [ddʒ] **gemo, fuggire**
[ts] [tts] **zio, pazzo**
[dz] [ddz] **Zerlina, mezzo**

Glides

[j] **pianto, patria, buio**
[w] **sguardo, sangue, tuoi**

Plosive Consonants

[b] [bb] **abate, babbo**
[p] [pp] **popolo, gruppo**
[d] [dd] **Alfredo, freddo**
[t] [tt] **tutore, tutto**
[g] [gg] **fuga, fuggo**
[k] [kk] **seco, secco**

Vibrant Consonants

[ɾ] [r] [rr] **caro, carta, carro**

Nasal Consonants

[n] [nn] **pane, fanno**
[m] [mm] **ama, mamma**
[ŋ] **fianco, languido**
[ɲ] [ɲɲ] **gnocchi, agnello**

Other Symbols

[:] lengthen preceding sound
['] syllabic stress
[‿] phrasal diphthong

Dictionaries

It is essential that the student acquire an Italian dictionary, but *caveat emptor*. Dictionaries vary greatly in the information they provide. The student for whom the pronunciation of the language is a major concern will need more than simple word translation from a dictionary.

Few Italian or Italian-English dictionaries use the IPA, but since Italian is phonetic (that is, spelling and sound are consistent) except for the letters *e*, *o*, *s*, and *z*, one needs only an indication for these letters. With the two vowels, unstressed *e*'s and *o*'s are considered closed and will therefore have no special indication. When they fall in the stressed syllable, closed *e*'s and *o*'s will usually have an acute accent and open ones will have a grave accent. Alternative symbols may be employed, such as a dot (.) underneath a stressed closed vowel and a cedilla (˛) under a stressed open vowel. Words with open vowels may be spelled with the IPA symbols [ɛ] and [ɔ].

With *s* and *z* the question is whether they are to be pronounced voiced or unvoiced. Usually the voiced sound is indicated by some symbol, such as a dot underneath; otherwise the unvoiced pronunciation is assumed. This is particularly essential for *z*, which is highly irregular.

Note that, although *n* before hard *c* [k] (as in **anche** [ˈaŋke]), hard *g* [g] (as in **sangue**) [ˈsaŋgwe], and *qu* [kw] (as in **dunque** [ˈduŋkwe]) assimilates to the sound [ŋ] (as in English **finger**), most Italian dictionaries do not indicate assimilations of *n*, either by using the phonetic symbol [ŋ] or any other symbols.

A good dictionary will also give appropriate verb forms if there is a change in vowel quality from the infinitive, for example, **prèndere** (**prési, préso**).

Finally, word stress must be indicated. It may be given for all words, but at the very least antepenult (third-to-last syllable) should be indicated (e.g., **ụmile, dẹbole**). If no indication is given, the assumption is the penult (second-to-last syllable) stress, or, in the case of final accented vowels, final syllable stress.

The student must make sure the dictionary he or she purchases provides the above information. If it does not, its use will be very limited.

Diacritical Marks

The grave accent (`) is the most commonly encountered diacritical mark in Italian. In older printed Italian it is always found with stressed final vowels in polysyllabic words. In modern printed Italian, stressed final *e* (when closed), *i*, and *u* often have the acute accent (´):

beltà vedrò lassù (or **lassú**) **partì** (or **partí**) **perchè** (or **perché**)

When stressed final *e* is open it will always have the grave accent: **caffè, ahimè.**

In three-letter monosyllabic words spelled consonant-vowel-vowel, the grave accent over the final vowel indicates that the first vowel is either a glide or a "softening" *i*:

più (or **piú**) **può piè diè già ciò**

Such words without an accent are to be pronounced as a diphthong:

pio tuo mie sia fia mai

(See sections "Glides" and "Diphthongs.")

The circumflex accent (ˆ) is very occasionally encountered in older Italian. It indicates that a letter has been omitted. It has no effect on pronunciation and its use is not obligatory:

dormîa (dormiva) odî (odii) côre (cuore)

The dieresis (¨) is sometimes found in musical settings when a glide is treated as a vowel: **vï-o-le**. It is also used in the name **Aïda** to indicate the unusual second-vowel syllabic diphthong [ai:] instead of the usual pronunciation of -ai- as [a:i].

The grave accent is also used to differentiate monosyllabic words that have different meanings but are otherwise spelled the same:

là (there)	**la** (the, it)
sè (oneself)	**se** (if)
è [ɛ] (is)	**e** [e] (and)
nè (or **né**) [ne] (nor)	**ne** [ne] (of it, of them)
sì (yes)	**si** (one, oneself)
dì (day)	**di** (of)

The same may occasionally happen with polysyllabic words: **àncora** ['aŋkora] (anchor), **ancora** [aŋ'ko:ra] (again). In polysyllabic words ending in *i* plus a vowel, the grave accent *may sometimes* be found over the *i* to indicate that the vowels form a diphthong (that is, the *i* is not a glide or softening *i*):

Lucìa [lu'tʃi:a] **magìa** [ma'dʒi:a] **follìa** [fol'li:a] **librerìa** [libre'ri:a]

Use of the accent in such cases is unfortunately inconsistent; these words are just as often found without accent. (See under "Glides.")

Syllabification

It is important to understand syllabification as an aid in determining relative length of vowel and consonant sounds. The following reflects the rules of orthographic (written) Italian. The spoken language differs somewhat from these rules as they relate to vowel length. (See "Vowel Length.")

A *single consonant* occurs between two vowels and begins the syllable with the following vowel:

a-mo-re po-po-lo fe-ri-to u-mi-le

A *double consonant* is two of the same consonant together. Syllables divide between the two consonants:

trop-po mat-to bel-lo car-ro

A *consonant cluster* is two or three different consonants together. The cluster will divide after the first consonant if it is *l, m, n,* or *r*:

al-tro tem-po con-tro par-la

and in a few rare cases where the consonant combination could not begin a word: **tec-ni-ca, ab-di-ca-re.**
   In all other cases the cluster belongs with the following vowel:

a-pri-re a-vrà la-dro fi-glio so-gno te-sta la-scia

Adjacent vowels are considered to be in the same syllable:

mio miei sua suoi mae-stro cie-lo Gio-van-ni

except when the second or third successive vowel-letter is a glide:

a-iu-to bu-io gio-ia muo-io ra-so-io

Second-vowel syllabic diphthongs, such as **maestro**, are virtually always given two notes by composers, giving the effect of two syllables. **Maestro** is then heard as **ma-e-stro**, a three-syllable word.
   More concerning adjacent vowels will be found under "Glides," "Diphthongs," "Triphthongs," and "Linking of Vowels between Words."

Word Stress

While musical settings usually make word stress clear, such is not always the case. Understanding patterns of word stress in Italian is important for understanding the character of the language.
   Most Italian words of two or more syllables take the stress on the penultimate (second-to-last) syllable (**parola piana** in Italian):

'Ro-ma Mi-'la-no Ve-'ne-zia Fi-'ren-ze

Some words take the stress on the final syllable (**parola tronca** in Italian). The final vowel will have either a grave or an acute accent:

bel-'tà per-'ché a-me-'rò par-'tí

Some words end in a final stressed diphthong. There is no accent:

co'lui   co'lei   ver'rai   an'drei

A large minority of words take the stress on the antepenultimate syllable (**parola sdrucciola** in Italian). Rarely is an accent given, so unknown words must be checked in a reliable dictionary:

'a-ni-ma	**'ti-mi-do**	**'la-gri-ma**	**'u-mi-le**
'te-ne-ro	**'ge-li-do**	**in-'co-gni-to**	**e-'ser-ci-to**

Certain recurring word endings result in the antepenult stress pattern. Some of them are:

Adjectives:	-*àbile* (**a'mabile, inesor'abile**)
	-*ìbile* (**pos'sibile, vi'sibile**)
	-*èvole* (**pia'cevole, ri'devole**)
	-*èsimo* (**ven'tesimo, undi'cesimo**)
Adjectives, Adverbs:	-*issimo* (**pre'stissimo, feli'cissimo**)
Nouns:	-*'udine* (**soli'tudine, abi'tudine**)
	-*logo* (**'prologo, ca'talogo**)
Verbs:	Many forms take the antepenult stress, particularly some infinitives in -*ere*, and third person plural forms: **'ridere, 'credere, 'amano, co'noscono, 've-dono, par'lavano**

A fourth-to-last-syllable stress (**parola bisdrucciola** in Italian) occurs in the third person plural of -*are* verbs that have an antepenult stress in singular forms:

dimenti'care	**di'mentica**	**di'menticano**
meri'tare	**'merita**	**'meritano**

and in some compound forms where pronouns are attached to verbs: **'portamelo** (bring it to me).

Apocopation

Apocopation or truncation (**troncamento** in Italian) is the elimination of (usually) the final vowel of a word. This happens frequently in literary Italian. The word stress does not change:

an'cor = **an'cora**   **a'mor** = **a'more**   **'aman** = **'amano**

Sometimes more than just the final vowel is removed:

san = 'sanno **dan** = 'danno **fan** = 'fanno

A family of Italian nouns has a complete form ending in *-de* and an apocopated form ending in a stressed vowel. The apocopated form is more common:

pietade = pietà	**piede = piè**	**fede = fe, fé, fè**
mercede = mercè	**beltade = beltà**	**virtude = virtù**
libertade = libertà	**amistade = amistà**	

In this excerpt from *La Bohème*:

v'entrar con voi pur ora / ed i miei sogni usati
e i bei sogni miei / tosto si dileguar

the words **entrar** and **dileguar** are apocopated forms of the third person plural of the past historic tense (*passato remoto*), **entrarono** (they entered) and **dileguarono** (they were dispersed), eliminating three letters. Confusion could arise because the apocopated form of the infinitive of these verbs is the same.

Other than words taken from foreign languages (including many proper names), the only Italian words that end in consonants are a few small words such as **il**, **con**, **per**, **non**, **nord**, **sud**, **est**, **ovest**, and contractions such as **del**, **nel**. *Any other word ending in a consonant does so as a result of apocopation.* It is incumbent upon the student to know the complete form of any apocopated word.

It is interesting to note that apocopation can only occur if the result is a final consonant of *l*, *m*, *n*, or *r*, the same consonants that can end a syllable. Thus **andiamo** can become **andiam** and **vanno** can become **van**, but **andate** cannot be altered.

Apocopation gives great flexibility to the Italian language for the purposes of adapting it to verse. Depending on the meter of the verse, a line of poetry can, for example, end in a stressed or unstressed syllable but employ the same word.

Vowels

Italian has five vowel-letters and seven vowel sounds. Some vowel-letters have additional functions.

1. The vowel-letter *a* always represents the sound [a]:
   cara ['kaːɾa], **amara** [aˈmaːɾa]
2. The vowel-letter *e* represents either the closed vowel sound [e] as in **vero** ['veːɾo], **stella** ['stella]; or the open vowel sound [ɛ], as in **prego** ['prɛːgo], **bella** ['bɛlla]

3. The vowel-letter *i* has three possible functions:
   The vowel sound [i]: **infinito** [infi'ni:to], **gigli** ['ʤiʎʎi]
   The glide [j]: **pietà** ['pjeta], **fiato** ['fja:to]
   Silent after *c*, *g*, and *sc*, when preceding another vowel (softening *i*):
   Giovanni [ʤo'vanni], **bacio** ['ba:ʧo], **lasciare** [la'ʃʃa:re]
   Also silent after *gl* when preceding another vowel:
   figlio ['fiʎʎo], **scegliere** ['ʃeʎʎere]
4. The vowel-letter *o* represents either the closed vowel sound [o] as in **voce** ['vo:ʧe], **sonno** ['sonno]; or the open vowel sound [ɔ] as in **sposa** ['spɔ:za], **donna** ['dɔnna]
5. The vowel-letter *u* represents either the vowel [u], as in **tuo** [tu:o], or the glide [w], as in **tuoi** [twɔ:i]

Vowel Length

Unlike German, in which closed vowel sounds are generally long and open vowel sounds are generally short, the quality and length of Italian vowel sounds are determined independently of each other.

Long vowels (indicated by [:]) are roughly twice as long as short vowels. Vowels are considered long when they occur in stressed open syllables. An open syllable is one that ends in a vowel.

amo ['a:mo]	**amare** [a'ma:re]	**amano** ['a:mano]
amavano [a'ma:vano]	**dolore** [do'lo:re]	**sospiro** [so'spi:ro]
sopra ['so:pra]	**padre** ['pa:dre]	

In stressed diphthongs and monosyllabic words with diphthongs, the first vowel is long:

amerei [ame'rɛ:i] **hai** [a:i] **poi** [pɔ:i] **aura** [a:ura]

There are some situations in which vowels in stressed open syllables are short:

- Stressed final vowels, including monosyllables:
  la [la], **amò** [a'mɔ], **amerà** [ame'ra]
- Before consonant clusters beginning with *s*: **testa** ['tɛsta], **posta** ['pɔsta] including *-sci* and *-sce* (considered doubled sounds): **lascio** ['laʃʃo], **pesce** ['peʃʃe]
- Before *-gli* and *-gn* (considered doubled sounds):
  egli ['eʎʎi], **ogni** ['ɔɲɲi]
- Before intervocalic *z* (single *z* considered doubled): spazio ['spattsjo], **letizia** [le'tittsja]

(See "Consonants" for explanation of consonant length.)

When pronouns are attached to verbs, the original vowel length remains:

amare [a'maːre]   **amarvi** [a'maːrvi]   **vedere** [ve'deːre]   **vedersi** [ve'deːrsi]

Stressed vowels occurring in closed syllables, that is, before double consonants, or before consonant clusters beginning with *l, m, n,* or *r* are short. The consonant following the short stressed vowel is long (see "Consonants"):

petto ['pɛtto]   **ricco** ['rikko]   **colpa** ['kolpa]
tempo ['tɛmpo]   **contro** ['kontro]

Unstressed vowels are always short, but they must remain pure.

It is again necessary to emphasize that although musical settings determine much about vowel length for singing, it is up to the singer to realize the subtleties of just when a sound begins and ends. The best way to achieve this in singing is to practice the inflections of the spoken language.

Specific Vowel Sounds

● **[a]**

The bright Italian [a] sound is often surprisingly difficult for English-speaking singers to find. The problems can be reduced to two:

1. *Italian* [a] *is brighter than its English counterpart.* English-speaking singers tend to center this vowel in the soft palate, which is often rather collapsed as well, giving it a darker, "lower" color. The Italian sound is oriented toward the hard palate, with the soft palate raised, and is consequently brighter and higher. While areas of register transition require the vocal technique to adjust vowel positions somewhat, this should not result in an unidiomatic vowel sound. The singer unused to this may feel that this [a] is "spread." The difference between "spread" and "bright" must be learned.

2. *In unstressed syllables,* [a] *must not lose its purity.* In English, vowels in unstressed positions almost always neutralize to [ə]. English speakers unwittingly carry this habit over into Italian (**Figaro** becomes **Fi-guh-ro**). This can be especially difficult in longer breath groups.

Practice the following recitative excerpts slowly, paying attention to the unstressed [a] sounds:

Le Nozze di Figaro, from Act II
... che l'avvertisca di certo appuntamento, che per l'ora del ballo a un amante voi deste.

Don Giovanni, from Act I
Era già alquanto avanzata la notte ...
... con una mano cerca d'impedire la voce, e coll'altra m'afferra stretta così, che già mi credo vinta.

● [i]

English has both closed [i] as in *seat* and open [I] as in *sit*. Italian has only the closed position for the vowel-letter *i*. It is easy for native English speakers to sometimes revert to the open position, making the Italian sound unidiomatic. Once again, it is in unstressed syllables that this tends to become an issue. In the word **finire** make sure that the first two syllables have the same vowel quality, and different length: [fi'niːre].

● [u]

English also has both closed [u] as in *boot* and open [U] as in *book*. Italian has only the closed position for the vowel-letter *u*.

The sound [u] is subject to great regional variation in English-speaking countries. This can present problems in singing this vowel sound. Usually the deviation from [u] involves a variation of the mixed vowel [y], as in French (**lune**) or German (**Bühne**).

When this situation is present, the tongue is tense at the back teeth where the tongue arches for [i], which distorts the [u]. The student should practice sustaining one pitch and alternating back and forth between [i] and [u], concentrating on how the tongue position changes. Moving from [i] to [u] should result in the arching of the tongue shifting from upper back teeth to oral pharynx. When the tongue is arched toward the oral pharynx, and the front of the tongue is relaxed, the result will be [u].

In addition, lip tension is often present, as if the singer were attempting to form the entire vowel [u] with the lips. Rounding of the lips is appropriate, but only by tensing the corners of the mouth. There should be no tension in the muscles of the lips.

crudo ['kruːdo]	**puro** ['puːro]	**duro** ['duːro]
Turiddu [tu'riddu]	**tutto** ['tutto]	**solitudine** [soli'tuːdine]
futuro [fu'tuːro]		

● [e], [ɛ], [o], [ɔ]

Open and Closed *e* and *o*

The sound [ɛ] occurs frequently in English (*bed, deck*) (but see p. 13 for differences between English and Italian). The closest English equivalent to the sound [e] normally occurs only as the first part of a diphthong (*maid, gate*). The sound [ɔ] occurs in English (*fought, awe*), while the sound [o] is only approximated as the first part of English diphthongs (*go, toe, blow*).

Because of the complexity of determining whether *e* is to be pronounced [e] or [ɛ], and whether *o* is to be pronounced [o] or [ɔ] in Italian, diction texts have had to devote a considerable amount of space to this point, giving the impression that it is perhaps the most important aspect of Italian diction. While certainly important, other aspects of Italian are more fundamental (for example, the purity of vowel sounds and appropriate articulation of single and double consonants) and should be perfected before spending a great deal of time learning the intricacies of open and closed *e* and *o*. For this reason, a detailed analysis of when stressed *e* and *o* are open or closed is relegated to the appendix.

Stressed Syllables versus Unstressed Syllables

In spoken Italian, the open pronunciation of the vowel-letters *e* and *o* occurs in the *stressed* syllable only, and then only sometimes: **bene** ['bɛːne] but **bere** ['beːre], **posta** ['pɔsta] but **posto** ['posto]. All *unstressed* *e*'s and *o*'s are therefore considered closed ([e] and [o]): **ridere** ['ridere], **ridono** ['ridono].

As a result, it is not possible for a simple word to have more than one open *e* or *o*. Compound words (not common in Italian) could have more than one. It follows that [e] and [o] far outnumber [ɛ] and [ɔ].

Notice how vowel quality can change with change of word stress: **bella** ['bɛlla], **bellezza** [bel'lettsa].

The sung language is approached somewhat differently. The Italian tradition of bel canto requires the singer to find the vowel position that will yield the most beautiful sound. With [a], [i], and [u] there is only one choice respectively (this does not include appropriate vowel modifications to which every singer must resort, notably in register transitions). With *e* and *o* the singer, in general and *within reason*, should favor whatever position on the spectrum of open to closed best suits that voice on a given pitch.

Various diction texts have dealt with this phenomenon in various ways. Some adopt the rules of spoken Italian without further explanation, while others recommend singing open [ɛ] and [ɔ] in some or all unstressed syllables. It has been customary for some pedagogues to require every unstressed *e* and *o* to be sung open. This approach is problematic on two counts:

1. Singers often over-open the vowels in a way that distorts the language. For example, the word **vedere** would be transcribed in this approach as [vɛˈdeːɾɛ]. If this word is sung on a single pitch in the middle voice with this pronunciation, it sounds very un-Italian. It is more appropriate to form all the vowels the same, the relative openness or closedness of the vowel determined by what sounds best in that voice on a given pitch.

2. The special nature of the open vowel in the stressed syllable is lost. The words **vogliono** [ˈvɔʎʎono], **possono** [ˈpɔssono], **muovono** [ˈmwɔːvono] all have open [ɔ] in the first, stressed syllable. If one sings these words on a single pitch in the middle voice following the recommendation to open the unstressed *o*'s as well, the vowel color of the stressed syllable loses its specialness.

A suitable approach is to treat IPA transcription of the sung language the same as that of the spoken language. In singing, however, it must be understood that *Italian closed e and closed o are not as closed as their counterparts in French and German*. The practical application of this for the singer is that, while French and German closed *e* and closed *o* are very near to the position of [i] and [u], respectively, Italian closed *e* and *o* are not. The open and closed positions of these vowels in Italian are very near to each other. Just as it is incorrect to overly open vowel sounds, it is also incorrect to overly close them.

Vocal considerations will often require approaches that may seem at odds with the strict application of the IPA symbol. Thus a tenor required to sing [ɛ] on a high A will necessarily have to sing it as he would [e], otherwise the tone would spread. A female voice singing [ɛ] in the lower middle range will also probably need to "cheat" toward [e] so that the tone remains focused. On the other hand, in full-voiced singing of Italian, middle voice [e] and [o] will be approached rather open, regardless of syllabic stress (more true of male voices than female, perhaps). This is where the singing of Italian most differs from the singing of French and German.

A further consideration is that the closed quality of a stressed *e* or *o* will subtly differ from that of an unstressed *e* or *o*. This is another fine point that the IPA cannot convey without resorting to a confusing array of symbols. The singer must be reasonably flexible in the vocal approach (though avoiding outright distortion) and not apply the "rules" too rigidly.

Another essential factor in all of this is the style of singing involved. In *recitativo secco* the distinction between open and closed will be greatest, since this style of singing is (or should be) very close to speech. The distinction will be less in *recitativo accompagnato*, and least in arias and other fully concerted music. In art song, one has to take into account the vocal requirements of the specific piece. An intimate, quiet song will likely more closely resemble speech, whereas a song requiring robust singing should be treated like an aria.

The thorny issue of determining when a stressed *e* or *o* is open or closed is one that takes much time to fully appreciate, but even then it is essential to have a reliable dictionary at hand. Basic patterns can (and should) be learned at the outset, but undue time should not be spent trying to memorize all the exceptions until more fundamental skills are perfected.

The appendix provides a thorough presentation of open and closed stressed *e* and *o*. It is to be used as a reference source and for continued study as the student becomes more proficient with Italian.

Appropriate Vocalization of [ɛ]

The comparison of [ɛ] between American English and Italian is similar to the comparison of [a]. The sound is common in English (*bed, said, spread*) but, just as with [a], the American pronunciation tends to be "back" and rather flat or low. In the languages of continental Europe this sound is generally pronounced with much greater height and forwardness.

American singers tend to position this vowel where they speak it, just as they do with [a]. Furthermore, American singers often equate this back position with vocal "space" and are reluctant to abandon the sensation. Indeed it often happens that when singers find a position for [ɛ] with appropriate lift and height, they mistakenly believe they are singing [e]. It is essential that the student learn to maintain lift and height in both [e] and [ɛ].

Inappropriate Diphthongs

The sounds [e], [ɛ], [o], and [ɔ] are likely to have an inappropriate diphthong when pronounced by English speakers: [e] and [ɛ] become [e:i] and [ɛ:I] and [o] and [ɔ] become [o:u] and [ɔ:U]. Italian **se** should not sound like English **say**; Italian **lo** should not sound like English **low**. When this problem is present the following points may be tried, individually or in combination, to help remedy the situation:

1. Assume the open position of the vowel.
2. Release the vowel (when final) with a slight aspiration.
3. Make sure that there is no movement of the jaw or lips in the transition of the vowel to the next sound.

Glides: [j] and [w]

A glide is a very short vowel sound that yields immediately to a longer vowel sound within the same syllable. The terms "semiconsonant" and "semivowel" mean the same as the term "glide."

Italian has two glides: [j] and [w]. The glide [j] (as in English *yes* [jɛs] and *music* ['mju:zIk]) is spelled in Italian with the letter *i*:

pietà [pje'ta]   **fiore** ['fjo:re]   **siamo** ['sja:mo]

It can also be spelled with the letter *j* (called "*i lungo*" in Italian). This spelling can only happen between vowels or at the beginning of a word; it cannot happen after a consonant:

Iago or **Jago** ['ja:go]   **aiuto** or **ajuto** [a'ju:to]   **muoio** or **muojo** ['mwɔ:jo]

The glide [w] (as in English *was* [wʌz] and *twenty* ['twɛntI] is spelled in Italian with the letter *u*:

cuoco ['kwɔ:ko]   **guerra** [gwɛrra]   **quattro** ['kwattro]

Vowel or Glide?

Because the vowel-letters *i* and *u* can function as vowels or glides, the proper function must be determined when these letters are followed by other vowels. This is one of the more difficult aspects of Italian.

In three-letter words like **tuo**, **pio**, **può**, **ciò**, the presence or absence of an accent gives this information. See "Diacritical Marks."

[w]

In polysyllabic words, *u* followed by a vowel is almost always a glide:

guardare [gwar'da:re]   **seguire** [se'gwi:re]   **iniquo** [i'ni:kwo]
fuori ['fwɔ:ri]

When *l* or *r* precedes *u* plus a vowel, the result is a second-vowel syllabic diphthong, in which the *u* functions as a short vowel rather than as a glide (see "Diphthongs"):

costruire [kos'trui:re]   **ruina** ['rui:na]   **Luigi** [lui:dʒi]

In Italian, *u* is never silent as in French **guide** [gi:d(ə)], **guerre** [gɛ:r(ə)], **languir** [lɑ̃gi:r].

[j]

Except for **io** [i:o], words beginning *i* plus vowel have [j]: **ieri** ['jɛ:ɾi], **Iago** ['ja:go]. In polysyllabic words, *i* followed by a vowel in the *interior* of a word is almost always a glide:

piano ['pja:no]   **bionda** ['bjonda]   **mestiere** [me'stjɛ:ɾe]   **chiuso** ['kju:zo]

The exceptions to the above are as follows:

- "Softening" *i*'s are silent:
  baciare [ba'tʃa:ɾe], **giovane** ['dʒo:vane]
- -*gli*- preceding a vowel has silent *i*: **sbaglio** ['zbaʎʎo]
- When the verb ending -*ano* follows *i*, the *i* is a vowel (part of a first-vowel syllabic diphthong) (see "Diphthongs"):
  siano ['si:ano] (also **sieno**), **fiano** ['fi:ano]
- The *i* functions as the first vowel in a second-vowel syllabic diphthong rather than a glide in the following situations: in most words beginning **ri-** plus vowel (usually a prefix: **riunione** [riu'njo:ne], **riamare** [ria'ma:ɾe], but also **rione** ['rio:ne]) and **di-** plus vowel (usually Greek-derived words like **dialetto** [dia'lɛtto], **diaframma** [dia'framma] - but not a word like **diavolo** ['dja:volo]); in **bi-** plus vowel when **bi-**, or **bio-** is a prefix (**bienne** ['biɛnne], **biografo** ['biɔ:grafo] but not **biondo** ['bjondo]); in the only word beginning **li-** plus vowel (**liuto** ['liu:to]); and in any word in which a consonant plus *l* or *r* precedes *i* plus a vowel (e.g. **trionfo** ['triɔnfo], **biblioteca** [biblio'tɛ:ka], **obliare** [o'blia:ɾe). See p. 122 for the same phenomenon in French.

[i:o] and [i:a] versus [jo] and [ja]

Confusion arises when a polysyllabic word *ends in i plus another vowel*. In such cases the *i* is sometimes a vowel, sometimes a glide, depending on the syllabic stress of the word: **Maria** [ma'ɾi:a], but **Mario** ['ma:ɾjo].

When the i is a vowel, it sometimes has an accent. This makes matters clear, but the practice is unfortunately not consistent: **Lucìa** or **Lucia** [lu'tʃi:a], **follìa** or **follia** [fol'li:a].

When the *i* is a glide, sometimes the vowel in the preceding syllable is spelled with an accent, but this is encountered even less often: **ària** or **aria** ['a:ɾja], **tragèdia** or **tragedia** [tra'dʒɛ:dja].

Musical settings will usually make the glide/vowel question clear. Nevertheless a reliable dictionary is essential for reference.

A few Italian words have the unusual formation of [w] plus [j] plus vowel. All are in the same syllable: **seguiamo** [se'gwja:mo], **quiete** ['kwjɛ:te].

Diphthongs

A diphthong is the occurrence of two adjacent vowel sounds in the same syllable. Sometimes a glide-vowel combination is called a "rising diphthong" and a vowel-vowel combination is called a "falling diphthong." For greater clarity and economy, glides are treated in the preceding section; this section will deal only with vowel-vowel diphthongs.

English pronunciation frequently requires diphthongs in syllables with only one vowel-letter (e.g., *by* [bɑːi]). Since Italian vowels are always pure, diphthongs must be spelled with two vowel-letters.

When the diphthong occurs in the stressed syllable, one vowel sound is longer than the other; that sound is called "syllabic." Usually the first vowel is syllabic (**aura** [ˈaːura]), but sometimes the second vowel is (**paura** [ˈpauːra]). Second-vowel syllabic diphthongs are virtually always set by composers as two syllables on two notes. See the section "Musical Settings of Diphthongs" later in the chapter.

In IPA transcription the syllabic vowel is followed by the colon [ː] if the vowel is long (e.g., **Paolo** [ˈpaːolo]). The syllabic vowel is underlined if it is short (e.g., **maestro** [ˈmaɛstro]). When the diphthong is in an unstressed syllable, both vowel sounds are approximately equal in length. Therefore no additional symbols are used (e.g., **aurora** [auˈrɔːra]).

Diphthongs occur frequently in Italian, much more so than in French and German. Here is a list of all twenty possible diphthong combinations (not all of which actually occur) with examples of first-vowel syllabic, second-vowel syllabic, and unstressed diphthongs where they occur in Italian.

Possible Diphthong Combinations	First-Vowel Syllabic	Second-Vowel Syllabic	Unstressed
ae	**aere** [ˈaːere]	**paese** [ˈpaeːze] **maestro** [ˈmaɛstro]	**maestà** [maeˈsta]
ai	**mai** [maːi] **avrai** [aˈvraːi]	**aita** [ˈaiːta] **Aïda** [ˈaiːda] **aire** [ˈaiːre]	**ahimè** [aiˈmɛ]
ao	**Paolo** [ˈpaːolo] **Menelao** [meneˈlaːo]	**faraone** [faˈraoːne] **Aosta** [ˈaosta]	**Taormina** [taorˈmiːna]
au	**aura** [ˈaːura] **causa** [ˈkaːuza]	**paura** [ˈpauːra] **baule** [ˈbauːle]	**aurora** [auˈrɔːra] **audace** [auˈdaːt͡ʃe]

Possible Diphthong Combinations	First-Vowel Syllabic	Second-Vowel Syllabic	Unstressed
ea	**idea** [i'dɛːa] **rea** [rɛːa]	**beato** ['beaːto] **teatro** ['teaːtro]	**realtà** [real'ta]
ei	**lei** [lɛːi] **vorrei** [vor:'rɛːi]	**inveire** [in'veiːre] **bey** [bei̯] (*L'Italiana in Algeri*)	**deità** [dei'ta]
eo	**trofeo** [tro'fɛːo] **Orfeo** [or'fɛːo]	**leone** ['leoːne]	**marmoreo** [mar'mɔːreo] **Leonora** [leo'noːra]
eu	**feudi** ['feːudi] **neutro** ['neːutro]	Does not occur	**Euridice** [euri'diːtʃe] **feudale** [feu'daːle]
ia	**mia** [miːa] **siano** ['siːano] **osteria** [oste'riːa]	Superseded by [j] glide as in **piano** ['pjaːno]	Usually [j] glide, but **diaframma** [dia'framma]
ie	**mie** [miːe] **gallerie** [galle'riːe]	Usually superseded by [j] glide, but **bienne** ['biɛnne]	Superseded by [j] glide as in **pietà** [pje'ta]
io	**mio** [miːo] **addio** [ad:'diːo] **periodo** [pe'riːodo]	Usually [j] glide, but **rione** ['rioːne]	Superseded by [j] glide as in **fiorito** [fjo'riːto]
iu	Does not occur	Usually superseded by [j] glide, but **liuto** ['liuːto]	Superseded by [j] glide as in **chiudete** [kju'deːte]
oa	**boa** [bɔːa]	**soave** ['soaːve] **cloaca** ['kloaːka]	**soavità** [soavi'ta]
oe	**eroe** [e'rɔːe]	**poeta** ['poɛːta]	**poesia** [poe'ziːa]
oi	**voi** [voːi] **poi** [pɔːi]	**gioire** ['dʒoiːre]	**ohimè** [oi'mɛ]
ou—Does not occur			
ua	**tua** [tuːa] **sua** [suːa]	Superseded by [w] glide as in **guardare** [gwar'daːre]	Usually superseded by [w] glide, but **ingenua** [in'dʒɛːnua]
ue	**tue** [tuːe] **sue** [suːe] **bue** [buːe]	Usually superseded by [w] glide, but **cruente** ['kruɛnte]	**assidue** [as'siːdue]
ui	**lui** [luːi] **cui** [kuːi] **altrui** [al'truːi]	Usually superseded by [w] glide, but **ruina** ['ruiːna]	Superseded by [w] glide as in **guidare** [gwi'daːre]
uo	**tuo** [tuːo] **suo** [suːo]	Superseded by [w] glide as in **fuori** ['fwɔːri]	Superseded by [w] glide as in **fuorché** [fwor'ke]

The most common diphthongs are:

- Those with first-vowel syllabic *i* (*-ia, -ie, -io*): **sia, mie, Dio**
- Those with first-vowel syllabic *u* (*-ua, -ue, -ui, -uo*): **sua, due, cui, tuo**
- First-vowel syllabic diphthongs ending in *i* (*-ai, -ei, -oi, -ui*): **mai, lei, voi, lui**
- and First-vowel syllabic *au*: **aula, aura, aumento, esaurito**

See the section "Musical Settings of Diphthongs" for a complete discussion.

Triphthongs

Strictly speaking, a triphthong is the occurrence of three successive vowel sounds in a word. Of course, three successive vowel-letters do not always result in a triphthong, even in Italian. If the first vowel-letter is an *i* after a *c* or *g*, as in **ciao** [tʃaːo], the i is silent and the result is a diphthong. In all other cases either the first or second vowel-letter must be a glide.

If the first vowel-letter is a glide, all three vowels are in the same syllable. This pattern is found in five common words:

tuoi [twɔːi] **suoi** [swɔːi] **vuoi** [vwɔːi] **puoi** [pwɔːi] **miei** [mjɛːi]

and occasionally in less common words: **quei** [kweːi], **guai** [gwaːi].

The glide-diphthong pattern can also be found as *-iai* [jaːi] in certain forms of verbs whose infinitives end in *-iare*: **studiare - studiai** [stuˈdjaːi].

If the second vowel-letter is a glide (this can only happen with [j]), the triphthong separates into two syllables. The syllables divide before the glide:

paio [ˈpaːjo] **buio** [ˈbuːjo] **aiuto** [aˈjuːto]

Four successive vowel-letters in a word result in one of two possibilities:

1. glide-vowel-glide-vowel, as in **muoio** [ˈmwɔːjo]
2. softening *i*-vowel-glide-vowel, as in **gioia** [ˈdʒɔːja]

Four successive vowel-letters always separate over two syllables.

See the section "Musical Settings of Triphthongs" for further discussion.

Consonants

Idiomatic rendering of Italian consonants is as important as that of the vowels. The proper rendering of each is often mutually interdependent.

Three basic points regarding Italian consonants must be mastered:

1. There must be a clear differentiation in the length of single and double consonants.
2. Consonants must be *unaspirated*; specifically *b*, *p*, *d*, and *t* release much less air than they do in English.
3. Consonants must be articulated *well forward*, more so than in English. Specifically, *d*, *t*, and *l* must be pronounced with the tongue in contact with the upper front teeth; the two *r* sounds must be mastered (flip and roll of the tongue).

It cannot be overemphasized how important these points are. If any of them is lacking, the Italian will sound unidiomatic no matter how well the vowels are pronounced.

IPA Rendering of Consonant Length

As discussed in the preface, the use of the symbol [:] to indicate length of sound is used differently in different texts, and sometimes it is not used at all. While it is fairly common among diction texts to use [:] for Italian double consonants, for example **gatto** ['gat:to], many dispense with it, including standard Italian publications on phonetics. The implication is that the two adjacent consonant symbols (e.g., ['gatto]) are sufficient to indicate extra length for the double *tt*. This text will follow this example and dispense with the colon. Certain consonant sounds that are long, but not orthographically doubled, are also treated variously in different texts. For example, the word **figlio** is often transcribed ['fiʎo], but other texts dealing with Italian phonetics transcribe this word as ['fiʎʎo]. The latter approach has the merit of consistency, since all long intervocalic consonant sounds are transcribed as doubled, as well as giving the visual reminder of length.

In addition to double consonants, then, the other intervocalic consonant sounds that are long will be transcribed as doubled in this text. They are:

- [ʎʎ]: **figlio** ['fiʎʎo], **meglio** ['mɛʎʎo]
- [ɲɲ]: **bagno** ['baɲɲo], **segno** ['seɲɲo]
- [ʃʃ]: **pesce** ['peʃʃe], **angoscia** [aŋ'gɔʃʃa]

At the beginning of a word, they are not doubled: **gli angeli** [ʎ'andʒeli], **sciolto** [ˈʃɔlto].

Intervocalic *z* is also considered doubled: **pazienza** [patˈtsjɛntsa]. See section "Individual Consonant Letters and Their Sounds," "z."

Single and Double Consonants

Clear execution of single and double consonants is one of the most important components of good Italian diction, spoken and sung. In no other language is the distinction so crucial.

A single consonant is always articulated as late and as quickly as possible, giving the vowels on either side of it maximum length. The importance of this cannot be stressed enough. English-speaking singers often have difficulty in doing this consistently in all situations.

Double consonants are always long, making the vowel preceding them shorter than it would be before a single consonant.

It is well known that Italian words are often differentiated solely by single and double consonants. Learning such word pairs is perhaps the clearest way to understand this phenomenon:

note [ˈnɔːte]	**notte** [ˈnɔtte]
sono [ˈsoːno]	**sonno** [ˈsɔnno]
Luca [ˈluːka]	**Lucca** [ˈlukka]
caro [ˈkaːro]	**carro** [ˈkarro]
fato [ˈfaːto]	**fatto** [ˈfatto]
casa [ˈkaːza]	**cassa** [ˈkassa]
m'ama [ˈmaːma]	**mamma** [ˈmamma]
fola [ˈfɔːla]	**folla** [ˈfolla]

Many Italian words have various combinations of single and double consonants in them. Practice these words with appropriate length for all vowel and consonant patterns:

capello [kaˈpello]	**cappello** [kapˈpɛllo]
adattare [adatˈtaːre]	**addiritura** [addiriˈtuːra]
affogare [affoˈgaːre]	**affollare** [affolˈlaːre]
correre [ˈkorrere]	**correte** [korˈreːte]
corretto [korˈrɛtto]	**chitarra** [kiˈtarra]
barattolo [baˈrattolo]	**barricata** [barriˈkaːta]

Double consonants are discussed in more detail beginning on page 32.

Individual
Consonant Sounds

Some consonant-letters in Italian are invariable in their sound and take the same IPA symbols as English. They are: *b* [b], *d* [d], *f* [f], *l* [l], *m* [m], *p* [p], *t* [t], *v* [v].

In pronouncing these sounds one needs to remember:

1. Whether they should be lengthened
2. That *b* and *p* require an unaspirated pronunciation
3. That *d* and *t* require an unaspirated and dental pronunciation
4. That *l* requires a dental pronunciation

English *b*, *p*, *d*, and *t* tend to be released with a considerable amount of air, especially *d* and *t* (more in some situations than others). Latin languages employ a much gentler release. Furthermore, if the tongue is not forward for *d*, *t*, and *l* the adjacent vowel sounds will be affected.

Singers are commonly admonished to bring the tip of the tongue in contact with the upper teeth to achieve the proper sound with these consonants. However, if only the tip of the tongue is employed, the base of the tongue can be tense. It is better to spread the tongue gently and bring the entire front of the tongue (not just the tip) in contact with the upper teeth. This will result in the proper consonant sound with minimal tension throughout the muscle of the tongue. A more relaxed tongue will not distort vowels.

A few more observations about [l]. Of the sounds that appear to be equivalent in English and Italian, this is perhaps the most problematic. English [l] is usually pronounced with the tongue rather tense and making contact with the palate well behind the teeth, as well as with a collapsed pharynx. Many students have such an ingrained English [l] position that it is very difficult for them to speak or sing an idiomatic Italian [l], especially a short intervocalic [l] as in **fatale**. The tongue must not only be forward, but there must be a vowel shape behind the tongue, either the vowel preceding or the vowel following the [l]. This will give the sound resonance as well as forwardness.

The following consonant-letters or combinations are either variable (that is, they can have more than one pronunciation) or require specific explanation because of their difference from English: *r*, *s*, *z*, *c*, *g*, *h*, *sc*, *gn*, *gli*, *nc*, *ng*, *nq*.

These letters and their sounds are discussed in the following section in the order just given.

Individual Consonant Letters and Their Sounds

● R

Italian *r* has two pronunciations:

1. Flipped—a single, quick stroke of the tip of the tongue against the front of the roof of the mouth
2. Rolled—two or more such strokes in rapid succession on a continuous release of breath

In both cases the sound is voiced, that is, the vocal folds are vibrating.

The preface to this book discusses the inconsistent use of IPA symbols for these sounds. Diction texts have traditionally used the following symbols for Italian:

- [ɾ] for intervocalic *r*, which may only be a flip
- [rr] for double *rr*, which may only be rolled
- [r] for all other occurrences of *r*, that is, as part of a consonant cluster, or beginning or ending a word. In these situations, the *r* may be flipped or rolled.

English speakers frequently have trouble with these sounds, since they do not occur in American English. Sometimes an individual can do one but not the other.

The traditional means for finding the flipped *r* is to substitute a *d*, executed with a quick stroke of the tongue. If it is done more lightly and more forward than normal English *d* requires, the tongue will be in essentially the same place as for flipped *r*. Try to use as little of the surface of the tongue as possible:

caro caro caro ['ka:do 'ka:do 'ka:do] becomes ['ka:ɾo 'ka:ɾo 'ka:ɾo]
vero vero vero ['ve:do 've:do 've:do] becomes ['ve:ɾo 've:ɾo 've:ɾo]

Pronouncing such *d*'s in quick succession while gradually reducing the amount of tongue involved usually enables the student to find the flipped *r*. Remember to *use only the tongue*. Do not move the jaw. It will inhibit the tongue and bring in elements of American *r*.

Once the flipped *r* is found, the rolled *r* can be practiced by repeating the flipped *r*. If the tongue can remain appropriately relaxed while doing this, it can achieve a "drum roll" effect, finding two or three flips with one effort of the tongue. Eventually a continuous roll of several seconds can be achieved. This requires a steady unforced air flow and a tongue free of undue tension.

As a single consonant between vowels, *r* is *always* flipped and *never* rolled:

vedere [ve'de:ɾe]   **amore** [a'mo:ɾe]   **diretto** [di'rɛtto]

As a double consonant, *rr* is *always* rolled and *never* flipped:

ferro ['fɛrro]   **aborrito** [abor'ri:to]   **bizzarro** [bid'dzarro]

Practice these potentially tricky words:

orrore [or'ro:ɾe]   **guerriero** [gwer'rjɛ:ɾo]   **irrorare** [irro'ra:ɾe]
correre ['korreɾe]   **Ferrara** [fer'ra:ɾa]   **Carrara** [kar'ra:ɾa]

The other possible contexts for *r* are:

- Beginning a consonant cluster:
  morte ['mɔrte], **fermare** [fer'ma:ɾe]
- Ending a consonant cluster:
  trenta ['trenta], **improvviso** [improv'vi:zo]
- Beginning a word: **roba** ['rɔ:ba], **ridere** ['ri:deɾe]
- Ending a word: **per** [per], **voler** [vo'le:r]

In general for the above four contexts, Italian speech employs the flip for nonemphatic situations and the roll for emphatic ones, although nonemphatic situations may also employ the roll. The heightened expressive nature of singing tends to use the roll most of the time, although parlando and recitative singing certainly could employ the flip.

● S

The letter *s* has two sounds (not including *sc*; see p. 28): unvoiced *s* and voiced *s*. Unvoiced *s* [s] occurs in these positions:

1. Beginning a word followed by a vowel:
   subito ['su:bito], **sorella** [so'rɛlla], **solo** ['so:lo]
2. Preceding an unvoiced consonant:
   stella ['stella], **testa** ['tɛsta], **squarcio** ['skwartʃo]
3. Following a consonant:
   senso ['sɛnso], **Alonso** [a'lonso], **forse** ['forse], **falso** ['falso]
4. Doubled (the sound is also prolonged):
   stesso ['stesso], **basso** ['basso], **assistere** [as'sisteɾe]

5. Final (rare, foreign words only):
Radamès [rada'mɛs], **Ramfis** ['ramfis], **Amneris** [am'neːris]

Voiced *s* [z] occurs in these positions:

1. Single between vowels:
sposa ['spɔːza], **tesoro** [te'zɔːro], **naso** ['naːzo]
2. Preceding a voiced consonant:
sgelo ['zʤɛːlo], **sguardo** ['zgwardo], **fantasma** [fan'tazma],
Amonasro [amo'nazro]

Italian dictionaries indicate that some words with intervocalic *s* use the unvoiced sound [s] in the Tuscan manner. The most common of these words are **casa, cosa, così,** and adjectives ending in **-oso** (-osa, -osi, -ose): **pietoso, curioso, doloroso.** Many Italians pronounce these words with a voiced *s* [z]. This practice is standard in sung Italian. It is recommended that every intervocalic *s* be pronounced as [z].

There are, however, three contexts in which *s* appears to be intervocalic, but functions as an initial *s* and is therefore unvoiced [s]:

1. When the reflexive pronoun **si** is attached to a verb:
vendesi (si vende) ['vendesi], **dicesi** (si dice) ['diːʧesi]
2. When the prefixes **ri-, di-,** and **tra-** occur before *s* plus a vowel: **riserva** [ri'sɛrva], **risorsa** [ri'sorsa], **disegno** [di'seɲɲo], **trasalire** [trasa'liːɾe]. This is also true of **pre-** when it is a prefix as in **preservare,** but not in other words such as **presente.** (Note the difference between **di-** as a prefix and **dis-** as a prefix. When the latter occurs before a vowel, the s is voiced:
disordine [di'zordine], **disonesto** [dizo'nɛsto])
3. Combinations with **sei** and **sette:**
ventisei [venti'sɛːi], **trentasette** [trenta'sɛtte]

● **Z**

The letter *z* has two sounds, voiced [dz] and unvoiced [ts]. These sounds are called "affricates," which means that two sounds are involved. This is reflected in the IPA rendering.

When it is intervocalic, *z* is pronounced as a double. IPA transcription reflects this, either [ddz] or [tts]. Double *zz* is always intervocalic and is, of course, always doubled. When initial in a word or as part of a consonant cluster, *z* is transcribed as a single consonant.

The voicing or unvoicing of z sounds in Italian is perhaps the most unphonetic aspect of the language. Guidelines for determining which sound is used in a given word are of limited help, although unvoiced z is much more common than voiced z. Unknown words should be checked in a reliable dictionary. The guidelines, such as they are, are as follows:

1. Intervocalic single z followed by i, usually (but not always) acting as a glide, is unvoiced:

   nazione [nat'tsjo:ne]   **benedizione** [benedit'tsjo:ne]
   grazia ['grattsja]   **pazienza** [pat'tsjɛntsa]
   polizia [polit'tsi:a]   **negozio** [ne'gɔttsjo]

2. Intervocalic single z not followed by i is voiced. This happens rarely, but it does occur in a number of proper names relevant to vocal repertoire:

   Suzuki [suddzu:ki]   **Azucena** [addzutʃe:na]
   Donizetti [donid'dzetti]

3. When z begins a word, it is *often* voiced:

   zero ['dzɛ:ɾo]   **zefiro** ['dzɛ:fiɾo]
   zerbino [dzer'bi:no]   **zimarra** [dzi'marra]
   zanzara [dzan'dzaɾa]   **Zerlina** [dzer'li:na]

   But many times it is unvoiced:

   zitto [tsit'to]   **zio** [tsi:o]   **zucchero** ['tsukkeɾo]   **zingaro** ['tsiŋgaɾo]

4. Apart from double zz, the most commonly encountered situation with z is after n. When this happens the z is usually unvoiced. *It is very common to hear these words mispronounced:*

   senza ['sɛntsa]   **stanza** ['stantsa]
   danza ['dantsa]   **costanza** [ko'stantsa]
   speranza [spe'ɾantsa]   **innanzi** [in'nantsi]
   silenzio [si'lɛntsjo]   **canzone** [kan'tso:ne]
   menzogna [men'tsoɲɲa]   **anzi** ['antsi]

   In a very few words, z after n is voiced:

   pranzo ['prandzo]   **bronzo** ['brondzo]   **bonzo** ['bondzo]
   gonzo ['gondzo]   **donzella** [don'dzɛlla]

5. When *z* follows *l* it is unvoiced:
   alzare [al'tsa:re], **calzone** [kal'tso:ne], **smilzo** ['zmiltso]
6. When *z* follows *r* it is usually unvoiced: **forza** ['fɔrtsa], **terzo** ['tɛrtso], **marzo** ['martso]; but sometimes voiced: **garzone** [gar'dzo:ne], **barzeletta** [bardze'letta]

● Double ZZ

Double *zz* can be voiced [ddz] or unvoiced [tts]. The only helpful guidelines are that certain common suffixes, such as **-ezza** and **-azza** (**-azzo**), are unvoiced, and that unvoiced double *zz* is much more common than voiced double *zz*.

Unvoiced zz

The following are some words with unvoiced *zz*:

nozze ['nɔttse]	**pezzo** ['pɛttso]
vezzo ['vettso]	**prezzo** ['prɛttso]
pozzo ['pottso]	**pazzo** ['pattso]
piazza ['pjattsa]	**razza** ['rattsa]
palazzo [pa'lattso]	**fazzoletto** [fattso'letto]
terrazza [ter'rattsa]	**bellezza** [bel'lettsa]
tristezza [tri'stettsa]	**ragazza(-o)** [ra'gattsa(-o)]
pizzicare [pittsi'ka:re]	**aguzzare** [agut'tsare]
ammazzare [ammat'tsa:re]	

Voiced zz

Some words with voiced *zz* are:

mezzo ['mɛddzo] (and derivatives **mezzogiorno, tramezzo,** etc.)

gazza ['gaddza]	**olezzo** [o'leddzo]
brezza ['breddza]	**gazzetta** [gad'dzetta]
bizzarra [bid'dzarra]	**azzurro** [ad'dzurro]
orizzonte [orid'dzonte]	**dozzina** [dod'dzi:na]
azzimato [addzi'ma:to]	**bizzeffe** [bid'dzɛffe]
lazzo ['laddzo]	

Also all verbs whose infinitives end in *-izzare* and their derivatives. This is the equivalent of English verbs ending in *-ize* (British *-ise*).

scandalizzato [scandalid'dza:to]	**realizzare** [realid'dza:re]
armonizzazione [armoniddza'tsjo:ne]	**agonizzare** [agonid'dza:re]

● C and G

Each of these two consonant-letters has two sounds (excluding *sc*, discussed later), a "hard" sound and a "soft" sound. The hard sound of *c* is [k]. The hard sound of *g* is [g].

The hard sound of each occurs when the consonant-letter is followed by the vowels *a*, *o*, or *u* or by a consonant (excluding *-gli* and *-gn*, discussed later).

canto ['kanto]	**come** ['ko:me]	**sicuro** [si'ku:ɾo]
credo ['kre:do]	**che** [ke]	**gatto** ['gatto]
gusto ['gusto]	**vago** ['va:go]	**streghe** ['stre:ge]
negletto [ne'glɛtto]		

When hard *c* and hard *g* are doubled, the sounds are prolonged as usual:

accanto [ak'kanto]	**fiocco** ['fjɔkko]	**ricche** ['rikke]
aggrada [ag'gra:da]	**veggo** ['veggo]	**fuggo** ['fuggo]

The "soft" sound of each of these consonant-letters is an affricate, or compound sound. Two IPA symbols are required. Soft *c* is [tʃ] as in English *ch* (chair). Soft *g* is [dʒ] as in English *j* (jump). The soft sound of each occurs when the consonant-letter is followed by *i* or *e*.

città [tʃit'ta]	**duce** ['du:tʃe]	**bacio** ['ba:tʃo]
cielo ['tʃɛ:lo]	**giro** ['dʒi:ɾo]	**giudice** ['dʒu:ditʃe]
gente ['dʒɛnte]	**giovane** ['dʒo:vane]	

In the case of the vowel-letter *i*, it is important to recognize whether it has a vowel function or whether it is silent, serving only to soften the *c* or *g*. Usually if the *i* is followed by another vowel it will be silent, as in **gioco** ['dʒɔ:ko], **caccia** ['kattʃa]. The exceptions are final stressed *-ia*, *-ie*, and *-io* as in **magia** [ma'dʒi:a], **bugie** [bu'dʒi:e], **leggio** [led'dʒi:o].

When soft *c* and soft *g* are doubled, the first sound of the compound is prolonged. In the case of soft *cc*, the tongue holds the [t] position, just as for double *tt*:

accidenti [attʃi'dɛnti]   **uccidere** [ut'tʃi:dere]   **eccellente** [ettʃel'lɛnte]

In the case of soft *gg*, the tongue holds the [d] position, just as for double *dd*:

oggi ['ɔddʒi]   **aggiungere** [ad'dʒundʒere]   **passaggio** [pas'saddʒo]

The following table organizes the sounds and spellings of *c* and *g* (for convenience, *e* and *o* are given only one sound apiece). Note that the letter *i* functions to soften an otherwise hard sound, and that the letter *h* functions to harden an otherwise soft sound.

[ka] *ca*	[ga] *ga*	[tʃa] *cia*	[dʒa] *gia*
[ke] *che*	[ge] *ghe*	[tʃe] *ce*	[dʒe] *ge*
[ki] *chi*	[gi] *ghi*	[tʃi] *ci*	[dʒi] *gi*
[ko] *co*	[go] *go*	[tʃo] *cio*	[dʒo] *gio*
[ku] *cu*	[gu] *gu*	[tʃu] *ciu*	[dʒu] *giu*

● H

The letter *h* is always silent in Italian. It can occur only in the following contexts:

1. After *c* and *g* to indicate the hard sounds of those consonant letters: **chiacchierare** [kjaˈkkjeˈraːre], **ghiaccio** [ˈgjattʃo]
2. In interjections such as
   ahi [aːi], **ahimè** [aiˈmɛ], and **ohimè** [oiˈmɛ]
3. As initial in a word. Other than in foreign words it occurs only in forms of the verb **avere**: **ho** [ɔ], **hai** [aːi], **ha** [a], **hanno** [ˈanno] (often apocopated to **han**). When one of these four words is preceded by another sound in the phrase, the preceding vowel or consonant will connect through the h to the next vowel with no lift or break: **non ho** [noˈnɔ], **che hai?** [keˈaːi], **egli ha** [eˈʎʎa], **cos'han?** [kɔˈzan].

Consonant Combinations and Their Sounds

● SC

When *s* precedes hard *c* it follows the voicing rules of *s* and is unvoiced.

scuola [ˈskwɔːla]   **esco** [ˈɛsko]   **scherzo** [ˈskɛrtso]   **boschi** [ˈboski]

When *s* precedes soft *c* a new combination is formed. The result is the sound [ʃ] as in English *sh*. Remember that when soft *sc* is intervocalic it is a long sound and is doubled in IPA transcription:

scendere [ˈʃɛndere]   **lasciare** [laˈʃʃaːre]   **sciogliere** [ˈʃɔʎʎere]

The following table organizes the sounds of *sc* in combination with all the vowel sounds. Compare with the table on p. 28. Once again, *i* is the softening letter and *h* is the hardening letter.

[ska] *sca* (**scarpa, tasca**)	[ʃa] *scia* (**lascia, sciagurato**)
[ske] *sche* (**scherno, tasche**)	[ʃe] *sce* (**pesce, scegliere**)
[ski] *schi* (**Schicchi, tedeschi**)	[ʃi] *sci* (**uscire, scimunito**)
[sko] *sco* (**fresco, scoprire**)	[ʃo] *scio* (**liscio, sciocco**)
[sku] *scu* (**scultura, scudo**)	[ʃu] *sciu* (**asciugare, sciupato**)

● GN

In Italian, as in French, the combination *gn* always results in the sound [ɲ]. The sound is the same as Spanish *ñ* as in **señor**, and similar to English [nj] as in **onion**. In English, however, two movements of the tongue are required, resulting in two sounds falling into two different syllables. In the other languages one tongue movement results in one sound, which always begins a syllable.

Intervocalically this sound in Italian is always long, indicated in IPA by doubling the symbol. The preceding vowel is always short.

sogno [ˈsoɲɲo] **signore** [siˈɲɲoːre] **legno** [ˈleɲɲo] **ogni** [ˈoɲɲi]

● GLI

The combination *-gli-* results in the sound [ʎ]. This sound is long and is rendered in IPA as a double (except when initial). Vowels preceding it are always short.

If the *i* is the only vowel-letter in the syllable, it will serve as the vowel [i]:

gli [ʎi] **figli** [ˈfiʎʎi] **egli** [ˈeʎʎi]

If the *i* is immediately followed by another vowel, the *i* is silent:

meglio [ˈmɛʎʎo]	**famiglia** [faˈmiʎʎa]
orgoglio [orˈgɔʎʎo]	**Guglielmo** [guˈʎʎɛlmo]

The sound is similar to English [lj] as in **valiant**, but English [lj] is considered two movements of the tongue and the two sounds are in different syllables. Italian [ʎ] is considered one movement of the tongue and always begins a syllable.

The word **gli** is the masculine plural article before words beginning with *s* plus a consonant (**gli studenti**), words beginning with *z* (**gli zii**), and words beginning with a vowel (**gli occhi**). In the latter case the *i* loses all vowel function, and the two words are pronounced as one: [ˈʎɔkki]. The spelling **gl'occhi** is often encountered in literary Italian, which more accurately suggests the proper pronunciation. It is incorrect to pronounce the *i* when **gli** is followed by a vowel, whether in the same word or in a different word.

gli uomini [ˈʎwɔ:mini]   **gli astri** [ˈʎ astri]   **quegli occhi** [kweʎˈʎɔkki]

The word **gli** also functions as the indirect object pronoun (to him, to it). It can be combined with a direct object pronoun to form **glielo** [ˈʎelo] and **gliela** [ˈʎela]. The *i* is silent.

Glielo darò—I will give it to him.

Very occasionally, *-gli-* is pronounced [gli]. This is most commonly encountered in the word **negligenza** [negliˈʤɛntsa] and its derivatives such as **negligente** [negliˈʤɛnte] and **negletto** [neˈglɛtto].

> *Lucia di Lammermoor*
> Fra poco a me ricovero darà negletto avello

● NC, NG, NQ

In spoken Italian, when *n* precedes hard *c*, hard *g*, or *q* within a word it assumes the sound [ŋ] as in English **sing** and **sink**. The following consonant retains its normal sound.

bianco [ˈbjaŋko]   **anche** [ˈaŋke]   **ancora** [aŋˈko:ra]
sangue [ˈsaŋgwe]   **inglese** [iŋˈgleze]   **dunque** [ˈduŋkwe]

It is common practice among Italian singers to sometimes pronounce *n* with its normal sound [n] in this context ([ˈduŋkwe] becomes [ˈdunkwe]). This is particularly so in slower, more sustained passages, where the more forward position of [n] is arguably more conducive than [ŋ] to the maintaining of the legato line, although the practice is not necessarily recommended. This alternative pronunciation to [ŋ] can lead to the insertion of a "ghost" vowel sound between the *n* and the following consonant (**dun-a-que**), which is most emphatically to be avoided, in spite of the fact that it is often heard from Italian singers.

Before soft *c* and soft *g*, *n* retains its normal sound.

incendio [inˈʧɛndjo]   **lanciare** [lanˈʧa:re]
ingiuria [inˈʤu:rja]   **ingegno** [inˈʤeɲɲo]

Other Possible Assimilations of N

Assimilation of *n* means that orthographic (written) *n* assumes a sound different from [n]. An example is the situation described above where orthographic *n* is pronounced [ŋ]. Two further assimilations of *n* are possible in Italian:

1. When *n* occurs before any of the three bilabial consonants *b*, *m*, and *p* (consonant sounds requiring lip closure), it may be pronounced [m]. While this is common in speech, it is much less common in singing, with its greater extension of sound over time. It is more likely to occur in *secco* recitative:

Il Barbiere di Siviglia

Don Bar - to - lo, Don Bar - to - lo! Don Ba - si - lio
[dom'bartolo] [domba'zi:ljo]

though it may occur in lyric singing when note values are short. When singing is more sustained, such assimilation is less likely, though certainly possible. If one singer chooses to do [un bɛl di], another may choose to do [um bɛl di]; both are valid.

2. A final possible context for assimilation of *n* is before [f] and [v] (labiodental sounds, requiring contact of upper teeth and lower lip). When *n* is assimilated before these sounds, the tongue does not come into contact with the hard palate, but is replaced by a "hum" in the position of the following [f] or [v]. The IPA symbol for this is [ɱ]: **un fior** [[un fjo:r] or [uɱfjo:r], **invano** [in'va:no] or [iɱ'va:no]. This text does not employ [ɱ] for Italian. While the singer certainly may use it when appropriate, the author is of the opinion that this sound is not necessary for idiomatic Italian.

PS, QU

The combination *ps* occurs at the beginning of certain Greek-derived words. As in German and French, but not in English, the *p* is lightly pronounced:

psicologia [psikolo'dʒi:a] **psichiatra** [psi'kja:tra]

The combination *qu* is pronounced [kw] as in English. The pronunciation of this combination is often confused with those of French and Spanish, which have no [w] glide:

questo ['kwesto]   **quel** [kwel]   **dunque** ['duŋkwe]

Characteristics of Double Consonants

While there are many categories for consonants (plosive, fricative, etc.), the following is sufficient for understanding proper execution of double consonants:

1. Consonants are either stop or continuing.
2. Consonants are either voiced or unvoiced.

The terms "stop" and "continuing" refer to air flow. Stop consonants require a momentary interruption of air flow by the tongue or lips; continuing consonants retain continuous air flow from the preceding vowel.

- Stop consonant sounds: [b], [d], [k], [g], [p], [t]
- Continuing consonant sounds: [f], [l], [ʎ], [m], [n], [ɲ], [r], [s], [ʃ], [v]

Certain sounds, for example [ŋ], [z], do not play a role in consonant doubling. [ʤ] and [dz] double the [d] while [ʧ] and [ts] double the [t].

"Voiced" and "unvoiced" refer to whether the vocal folds are vibrating in pronouncing the consonant. Many consonant sounds can be paired with another as two versions of the same sound, the only difference being that one is voiced and one is unvoiced:

- Voiced: [b], [d], [g], [v], [z], [ʤ], [dz]
- Unvoiced: [p], [t], [k], [f], [s], [ʧ], [ts]

The four unpaired consonants, all voiced, are [l], [m], [n], and [r] ([ʎ] is a variation of [l] and [ɲ] is a variation of [n]). These are the same four consonants encountered previously as the ones that can end syllables and apocopated words in Italian.

Because double consonants are lengthened, the singer must be particularly aware of the appropriate characteristics of the consonant. This may cause some difficulty at first. For instance, the singer unused to articulating a double *tt* as in **fatto** is often initially uncomfortable with the length of time the air is not moving and the vocal folds are not vibrating, since these traits seem antithetical to singing. With stop double consonants, moreover, the release must not be accomplished by forcing the air. Double consonants are not more forceful than single consonants, just longer. The student must learn that these characteristics are as important to good Italian as anything relating to vowels.

Here is a summary of all Italian double consonants grouped by their particular characteristics:

Unvoiced stop	[kk]	spelled cc, **peccato** [pek'ka:to], **ricco** ['rikko] spelled cq, **acqua** ['akkwa], **acquisto** [ak'kwisto] spelled qq, **soqquadro** [sok'kwa:dro]
	[pp]	**troppo** ['trɔppo], **eppure** [ep'pu:re]
	[tt]	spelled tt, **letto** ['letto], **carattere** [ka'rattere] spelled cc [ttʃ], **caccia** ['kattʃa], **succedere** [sut'tʃɛ:dere] spelled zz [tts], **pozzo** ['pottso], **carezza** [ka'rettsa]
Unvoiced continuing	[ff]	**buffa** ['buffa], **affanno** [af'fanno]
	[ss]	**stesso** ['stesso], **passato** [pas'sa:to]
	[ʃʃ]	**uscire** [uʃ'ʃi:re], **ascendere** [aʃ'ʃɛndere]
Voiced stop	[bb]	**gobbo** ['gɔbbo], **ubbidire** [ubbi'di:re]
	[dd]	spelled dd, **freddo** ['freddo], **Maddalena** [madda'lɛ:na] spelled gg [ddʒ], **peggio** ['pɛddʒo], **fugge** ['fuddʒe] spelled zz [ddz], **mezzo** ['mɛddzo], **bizzarro** [bid'dzarro]
	[gg]	**veggo** ['veggo], **protegga** [pro'tɛgga]
Voiced continuing	[ll]	**folle** ['fɔlle], **uccello** [ut'tʃello]
	[ʎʎ]	**egli** ['eʎʎi], **foglio** ['fɔʎʎo]
	[mm]	**dimmi** ['dimmi], **ammazzare** [ammat'tsa:re]
	[nn]	**sonno** ['sonno], **condannata** [kondan'na:ta]
	[ɲɲ]	**sogno** ['soɲɲo], **maligno** [ma'liɲɲo]
	[rr]	**ferro** ['fɛrro], **orrore** [or'ro:re]
	[vv]	**ovvio** ['ɔvvjo], **davvero** [dav've:ro]

Articulating Double Consonants in Singing

In musical settings, exact vowel length is of course largely determined by the length of the note as well as by what consonants follow it. A *long* note will always have a long vowel, but if it is followed by a double consonant the vowel will be shortened at the end of the note. A *short* note involving a double consonant will be approximately half vowel and half consonant.

The following excerpt from *Don Giovanni* is notated in the score thus:

Bat - ti   bat - ti,o   bel   Ma - set - to
['batti 'battjo bɛl mazetto]

Here is the rhythm rewritten to illustrate how the double *tt*'s should be articulated, stopping the consonants on the tied notes as indicated:

Bat - ti   bat - ti,o   bel   Ma - set - to

As an example of a double consonant at the end of a long note, this excerpt from Donaudy's song *Vaghissima sembianza* is notated:

V'ha   ri - trat - ta
[va ri'tratta]

The double *tt* at the end of the long note should be executed like this (occurring on the final tied note):

V'ha   ri - tra - t - ta

While there is a certain artificiality in placing the double consonant in a precise rhythm, it is an excellent means by which the inexperienced singer can get a sense of how to execute double consonants. When the skill is developed the crutch can be abandoned.

Phrasal Doubling

In Italian, a word beginning with a consonant may have that consonant pronounced as if it were a double if the preceding word ends in a vowel. This phenomenon is commonly pointed out by Italian phoneticians (**raddoppiamento sintattico** in Italian), and is called "phrasal doubling," or by the technical term "phrasal sandhi." It can occur in the following situations:

1. After most monosyllabic words, but *not* articles (**la, le, lo, gli, i**) or pronouns (**la, le, lo, li**)

2. After a polysyllabic word ending in a final stressed vowel
(e.g., **perché**)
3. After certain two-syllable words, specifically **come**, **contra**,
dove (**ove**), **qualche**, and **sopra** (**sovra**)

Phrasal doubling can clearly be seen in some words whose
spellings have changed to reflect it:

chissà from **chi sa**   **giammai** from **già mai**
sissignore from **sì signore**   **davvero** from **da vero**
ebbene from **e bene**   **dammi** from **da mi**

In older Italian, and even in some relatively modern poetic Italian, one encounters spellings without the double consonants that
are found in modern Italian spelling: **de la** for **della**, **a Dio** for **ad-
dio**. Because of the phenomenon of phrasal doubling, these combinations should be pronounced as doubles no matter what the
spelling.

E'l ven-to su   la   fron - da   *La Serenata (Tosti)*
[el 'vɛnto 'sulla 'fronda]

There is not uniform agreement among the experts about all
the details of when phrasal doubling applies. It is a potentially
strong expressive device in singing, but the moderately experienced
singer should treat it with caution and not overdo it. Do not consider it a necessity but rather an option. Listen carefully to Italian
singers (and speakers) and observe what they do.

Some examples of possible phrasal doubling:

a me [am'me]   **da te** [dat'te]
fra poco [frap'pɔ:ko]   **che fai** [kef'fa:i]
ma via [mav'vi:a]   **ho paura** [ɔp'pau:ɾa]
sarà buono [saɾab'bwɔ:no]   **dove vai** [dovev'va:i]
so tutto [sot'tutto]   **va bene** [vab'bɛ:ne]
se fosse [sef'fosse]   **come lui** [komel'lu:i]

Consonant Clusters

When [l], [m], [n], [ŋ], and [r] begin a consonant cluster, their sounds
are lengthened like double consonants. Use of the colon [:] or doubling of the IPA symbol in these cases would seem logical, but it is

not standard. Remember that the preceding vowel is short, and the subsequent consonant (part of the same syllable) is arrived at quickly:

colpa ['kolpa]   **tempo** ['tɛmpo]   **donde** ['donde]
porta ['pɔrta]   **sangue** ['saŋgwe]

Failure to pronounce these sounds with enough vocal resonance, enough forward placement of the tongue, or simply enough energy is very common among singers inexperienced with Italian. The initial sound of the cluster is therefore muffled or lost altogether, compromising clarity of text and expressiveness of singing.

For English speakers this is particularly true when the cluster is preceded by [a]. The tendency to pronounce [a] too darkly, combined with the tendency to position the tongue too far back for [n] and especially for [l], often results in serious distortion in such words. Practice these words, keeping the [a] bright and the consonants forward:

caldo ['kaldo]   **altro** ['altro]   **saltare** [sal'taːre]
santo ['santo]   **quanto** ['kwanto]   **campo** ['kampo]

In musical settings calling for a long note on a vowel followed by a consonant cluster, the first consonant of the cluster may be somewhat anticipated, both to imply a shorter vowel sound and to give expressive length to the consonant sound. This is similar to treatment of double consonants, already discussed. The extent to which this is done will vary according to context.

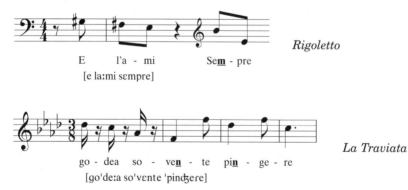

E   l'a - mi   Se**m** - pre
[e laːmi sɛmpre]

Rigoletto

go - dea so - ve**n** - te pi**n** - ge - re
[go'deːa so'vɛnte 'pindʒere]

La Traviata

When _r_ ends a syllable it may be rolled or flipped, though in singing it is usually rolled (see the section dealing with _r_, beginning on p. 22). Whether to roll and how long to roll depend on the dramatic/emotional intensity of the moment.

While expressive lingering on the first sound of a consonant cluster is a device that can lend appropriate color to the Italian language, it should be treated with care. It should not be overdone.

Word Underlay in Scores

In musical scores, the placement of Italian words under notes to be sung is often highly misleading in terms of which syllables should be sung on which notes. One example is from a score of *L'Elisir d'Amore*:

In o - gni ar - te è pro - fes - sor
[in 'oɲɲ'artɛ profes'soːr]

This is to be performed (and should be notated):

In o - gni ar - te è pro - fes - sor

Another example is from a score of *Le Nozze di Figaro*:

non l'ha il Con - te a - bo - li - to?
[non laįl 'kont eabo'liːto]

The double rhythmic notation is for the Italian original and the English translation. Although the second eighth note of the full measure is for the English translation only, the second syllable of **conte** is placed directly beneath it, giving the impression that the syllable should be placed there. The proper notation of the Italian text with Mozart's notes is:

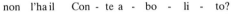

non l'ha il Con - te a - bo - li - to?

A similar example comes from a score of *Così fan tutte*:

(ma non) voglio a - ver col - pa   se poi   nasce   un im - broglio
[ma non 'voʎʎo‿a'veːr 'kolpa se pɔi 'naʃʃe‿un im'brɔʎʎo]

A more appropriate notation is:

se poi na - sce un im - bro - glio

Misleading word underlay is very common. The text must be spoken to find the proper linking of sounds, which then must be placed in the given rhythm.

Musical Settings of Diphthongs

Under "Syllabification" it has been explained that diphthongs are considered to be in one syllable. This can be seen in innumerable musical settings in which composers set first-vowel syllabic diphthongs to one note:

Il **mio** te - so - ro in - tan - to   *Don Giovanni*
[il miːo teˈzɔːro inˈtanto]

Diphthongs are also set to two or more notes, just as any syllable can be, but the frequent setting of diphthongs to one note is one indication that they are heard as a single syllable.

Second-vowel syllabic diphthongs are virtually always separated by composers over two notes:

So - **a** - ve sia il ven - to   *Così fan tutte*
[ˈsoaːve siːa ͜ il ˈvɛnto]

although very occasionally they are set to one note:

Don Ba - si - lio, mio **mae** - stro di can - to   *Le Nozze di Figaro*
[dom baˈziːljo miːo ˈmaɛstro di ˈkanto]

Unstressed diphthongs are treated similarly to first-vowel syllabic diphthongs. Single-note setting is very common, but the two vowel sounds are also frequently separated over two notes:

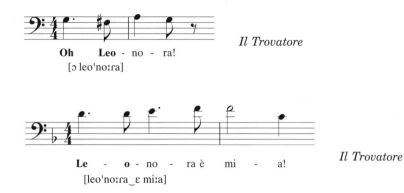

Oh **Leo** - no - ra!   *Il Trovatore*
[ɔ leoˈnoːra]

Le - **o** - no - ra è   mi - a!   *Il Trovatore*
[leoˈnoːra‿ɛ miːa]

Here are some representative examples of diphthongs set by composers to one note:

a   **cui**   tri - bu - ta in - cen - si   *Le Nozze*
[a kuːi triˈbuːta‿inˈtʃɛnsi]   *di Figaro*

no - me   di   **lui**   si a -   ma - to   *Rigoletto*
[ˈnoːme di luːi si‿aˈmaːto]

la   **tua**   fie - rez - za   *Sebben crudele (Caldara)*
[la tuːa fjeˈrettsa]

al   **mio**   duo - lo   *Le Nozze di Figaro*
[al miːo ˈdwɔːlo]

(e innamo) - ran - do **l'aer** an - te - lu - ca - no   *Falstaff*
[e‿innamoˈrando laːer anteluˈkaːno]

Lucia di Lammermoor

mi col - pi di **sua** vo - ce!
[mi kol'pi di suːa 'voːtʃe]

Il Barbiere di Siviglia

Al - l'i-**dea** di quel me - tal - lo
[alli'deːa di kwel me'tallo]

Vanne, o rosa fortunata (Bellini)

non a - **vria** più bel con - ten - to
[non a'v'riːa pju bɛl kon'tɛnto]

Diphthongs: Vowel Distribution in Singing

Distribution of vowel sounds in first-vowel syllabic diphthongs set to one note usually results in one of two possibilities:

1. The stressed vowel receives the majority of the note value, with the unstressed vowel occurring late in the note:

O del mio dolce ardor (Gluck)

L'au- ra che tu re - spi - ri
['laːura ke tu re'spiːri]

Il Trovatore

Il ba - len del **suo** sor - ri - so
[il ba'leːn del suːo sor'riːzo]

2. The two vowel sounds receive approximately equal time (although the syllabic vowel remains stressed). This is often the case with shorter note values:

Il Trovatore

Sper - da il so - le d'un **suo** sguar - do
['spɛrda‿il 'soːle dun suːo 'zgwardo]

Sometimes when a first-vowel syllabic diphthong occurs on a note of long duration, the first vowel may yield to the second vowel rather soon, so that the second vowel takes more of the note value. This is not obligatory, but the result may be more effective. In such cases the first, syllabic vowel must be strongly stressed for proper comprehensibility of the word.

Don Pasquale

Pria di par - tir, si - gno - re
['priːa di partiːr]
or ['priaː]

Otello

O - ra e per sem - pre ad - **dio** san- te me- (morie)
['oːra‿e per 'sɛmpre ad'diːo]
or [ad'dioː]

La Traviata

ve - dea schia - vo cias - cun di **sua** bel - lez - za
[ve'deːa 'skjaːvo tʃas'kuːn di suːa bel'lettsa]
or [suaː]

As these examples demonstrate, there is often no single correct solution to vowel distribution, and subtle variations as to the precise moment of vowel change are among the devices that give expressive color and nuance to the Italian language.

It is often suggested that the note on which the diphthong occurs should be divided into smaller note values to reflect the distribution of the vowel sounds over the note:

Amarilli (Caccini)

[ama'rilli ɟil miːo‿a'moːre]

While this can be useful at an initial stage, it is extremely important that such a subdivision not be heard as separate notes. If a composer wishes to set a diphthong to more than one note, the composer will do so, and often does. If a composer chooses to set a diphthong to one note it must sound as one; the transition must be very smooth. In the end, the vowel transition *should have no strongly rhythmic character*.

When a first-vowel syllabic diphthong is slurred over two or three notes, the second vowel sound will fall on the final note, unless slur markings indicate otherwise:

Lucia di Lammermoor

[la pje'taːde in suːo fa'voːre]

Il Trovatore

[del miːo kɔːr]

If there are four or more notes in a moderate to fast tempo, changing the vowel on the second-to-last note is advisable:

L'Elisir d'Amore

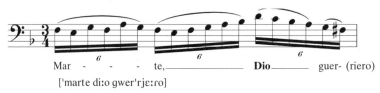

['marte diːo gwer'rjeːro]

Il Trovatore

d'un   **suo**———————— sguar - do

[dun suːo 'zgwardo]

unless the second vowel is weak (*i* or *u*), when it should go on the final note:

Lusinghe più care (Handel)

(invo)-la   -   te   l'al - **trui**———— li - ber-(tà)

[invoˈlaːte lalˈtruːi liberˈta]

but the composer may indicate vowel division by specific slur markings:

Il Trovatore

(fa) vel - li in   **mi**   -   **o**———— fa - vor

[faˈvɛlli‿in miːo faˈvoːr]

Linking of Vowels Between Words: Phrasal Diphthongs

Most Italian words end with a vowel; many begin with a vowel. Consequently many words are linked by contiguous vowel sounds. This is one of the primary elements in the legato flow of the language, spoken as well as sung.

In musical settings, when words within a phrase meet in this way the vowels connecting the words usually receive one note. The result is sometimes called a "phrasal diphthong" or "phrasal triphthong." To the inexperienced eye, it often looks as if there are not enough notes for the number of syllables:

I Puritani

ripiombarlo agli a - bissi in e   -   terno

Non-Italian scores will sometimes indicate phrasal diphthongs with the symbol ‿, but the practice is not consistent. Italian scores do not do this, assuming the (presumably Italian) reader will understand how to connect words in this way. The singer must learn to recognize phrasal diphthongs and triphthongs and determine to which note they are applied. See the section "Word Underlay in Scores."

Vowel Distribution in Singing Phrasal Diphthongs

Singers often do not accurately execute the phrasal diphthong set to one note. Improper execution results in the addition of a note.

Don Giovanni

Le Nozze di Figaro

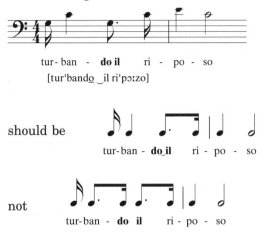

tur- ban - **do il** ri - po - so
[tur'band<u>o</u> ⌣ il ri'poːzo]

should be

tur- ban - **do͜il** ri - po - so

not

tur- ban - **do il** ri - po - so

Once it is determined which note takes the phrasal diphthong, the singer must determine how much of the note value to give to each vowel sound. When the phrasal diphthong occurs on a short note value, the two vowel sounds are given approximately equal time, as with ordinary diphthongs.

Vaga luna (Bellini)

El- **la è** sol, si, el- **la è** sol nell' av - ve - nir.
['ella͜ɛ soːl si 'ella͜ɛ sol nellavve'niːr]

Care selve (Handel)

ven - **go in** trac - cia del mio cor
['vɛŋgo͜in 'trattʃa del miːo kɔːr]

It is when the note value is longer that it becomes necessary to determine the relative length of vowel sounds. The following guidelines are offered to help this process:

1. Two of the same vowel-letter sound as one:

Vittoria, mio core (Carissimi)

Già l'em- **pia a'** tuoi dan - ni
[dʒa 'lɛmpja twoːi 'danni]

45

Le Nozze di Figaro

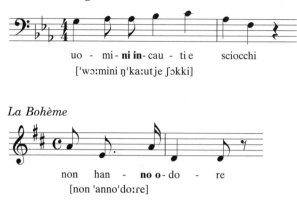

uo - mi - **ni in**-cau - ti e   sciocchi

['wɔːmini ŋ'kaːutje ʃɔkki]

La Bohème

non   han -   **no o**-do   -   re

[non 'anno'doːre]

2. The most common phrasal diphthongs consist of two un-stressed vowels. When this happens with combinations of *a, e,* and *o* (the so-called strong vowels), the *second* will usually be longer, as if in anticipation of the stressed syllable of the second word:

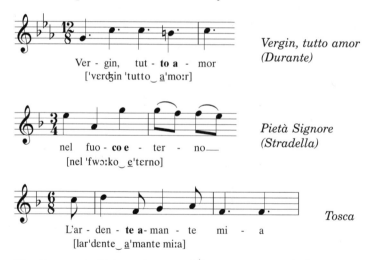

Ver - gin,   tut - **to a** - mor

['verʤin 'tutto‿ a'moːr]

Vergin, tutto amor
(Durante)

nel   fuo - **co e** - ter - no——

[nel 'fwɔːko‿ e'tɛrno]

Pietà Signore
(Stradella)

L'ar - den - **te a**- man - te   mi - a

[lar'dɛnte‿ a'mante miːa]

Tosca

The frequent elision of some of these unstressed phrasal diphthongs reflects the relatively greater importance of the second vowel: **quest'amplesso, Donn'Elvira.**

3. When *i* and *u* are unstressed, they are usually short and weak in the phrasal diphthong, regardless of their position in the phrasal diphthong. This is more apparent in singing than in speech:

Come raggio di sol (Caldara)

di   gio-**ia un** lab- **bro in** - fio - ra

[di ʤɔːja‿ un labbro‿ infjoːra]

I Pagliacci

fac - **cia in** - fa - ri - na
['fatʃa_infaˈriːna]

Un Ballo in Maschera

la sua pa - ro - **la u** - drà
[la suːa paˈrɔːla_ uˈdra]

4. Initial unstressed *i* will usually become [j], including before *u*:

Ed in - spi - **ri, ed** in - spi - **ria** - glie - le - men-ti   *Vaga luna (Bellini)*
[edinˈspiːrjedinˈspiːrjaʎʎeleˈmenti]

Vie - **ni o** - ve a - mo - re   *Le Nozze di Figaro*
[ˈvjɛːnjˈoːve a̯ˈmoːre]

ti pren-**di un** al - tro a - man - te   *La Bohème*
[ti ˈprendj un ˈaltro̯ a̯ˈmante]

5. Initial unstressed *i* after *c* or *g* becomes virtually silent:

Por - **gi, a** - mor—   *Le Nozze di Figaro*
[ˈpɔrdʒ aˈmoːr]

e tu non sor - **gian** - co - ra   *Il Barbiere di Siviglia*
[e tu non ˈsordʒ aŋˈkoːra]

6. When a stressed vowel occurs before an unstressed vowel, the first, stressed vowel will take more of the note value. This includes the words **a**, **o**, **e**, and **è**, the so-called "stressed monophthongs." Such occurrences are rare:

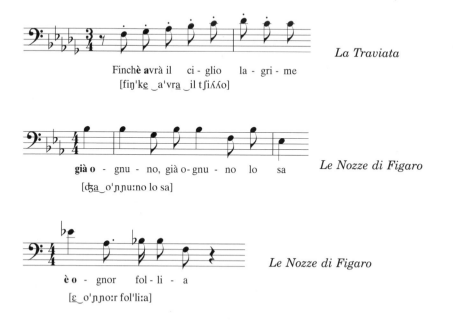

Finchè **a**vrà il   ci - glio   la - gri - me   *La Traviata*
[fiŋ'ke ‿a'vra ‿il tʃiʎʎo]

già o - gnu - no, già o-gnu - no   lo   sa   *Le Nozze di Figaro*
[dʒa ‿o'ɲɲuːno lo sa]

è o - gnor   fol - li - a   *Le Nozze di Figaro*
[ɛ ‿o'ɲɲoːr fol'liːa]

Sometimes special circumstances require exceptions to the above guidelines. For example, the word **tu** may be stressed within the phrase and therefore the [u] will be long if set as part of a phrasal diphthong:

tu a   -   scen - de-re il   *La Bohème*
[tu ‿a'ʃʃɛndere]

Non   hai   tu in   Men - fi   *Aïda*
[non aːi tu ‿in mɛnfi]

When the singer is executing a tenuto or a fermata, or even is just stretching a phrase on a phrasal diphthong, it is often desirable for the singer to remain on the first vowel, even if the guide-lines suggest otherwise: **son tranquilla e lieta** would normally be [soːn traŋ'kwilla‿e 'ljɛːta], but in Puccini's setting it may be prefer-able to sing [soːn traŋ'kwilla‿e 'ljɛːta].

La Bohème

Son tran - quil - **la e** lie - ta

Similarly, **fida e costante** ['fiːda‿e ko'stante] becomes ['fiːda‿eko's-tante]:

*Il Barbiere
di Siviglia*

(a) - man - te che fi - **da e** co - stante

In addition, there are various situations in which the rigid ap-plication of the above guidelines does not necessarily yield the best result. In this example it seems preferable to make [i] stronger within the phrasal diphthong (exception to no. 3 above):

Tor - na, ca- ro **i** - de - al⸻

['torna 'kaːro‿i'deaːl]

Ideale (Tosti)

These long-note phrasal dipthongs seem to work better if the first vowel is longer (exception to no. 2):

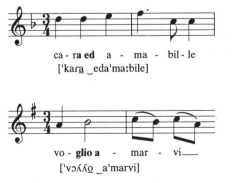

ca - **ra ed** a - ma - bil - le

['karaˌ‿eda'maːbile]

Ombra mai fu (Handel)

vo - **glio a** - mar - vi⸻

['vɔʎʎoˌ‿a'marvi]

*Per la gloria d'adorarvi
(Bononcini)*

I Capuleti ed i Montecchi

O quan - te vol - **te, o** quan - te

[ɔ 'kwante 'vɔlte ‿o kwante]

In Donna Elvira's opening scene in *Don Giovanni*, two stressed monophthongs (the word **e** and the word **a**) occur on a single half note. Equal distribution would make the half note sound like two quarter notes. The best solution is to shift vowels fluidly either just before or just after the second beat:

Don Giovanni

e a me non tor - na an - cor

[e̯ ‿a me non 'tornaŋ'koːr]

While the guidelines for vowel distribution in phrasal diphthongs should be studied and understood, these exceptions demonstrate that there is considerable room for variance. Once again, there is often no single correct solution. It is important for the student to develop an ear for the cadence of the language, and then apply musical common sense.

Musical Settings of Triphthongs

Monosyllabic words with triphthongs are often set to one note. The first vowel-letter is a glide and the second is the syllabic vowel. The final vowel is very late and very short:

Aïda

Vin - ci - tor de' **miei** fra - tel - li

[vintʃi'toːr de mjɛːi fra'tɛlli]

Malinconia, ninfa gentile (Bellini)

I **tuoi** pia - ce - ri

[i twɔːi pja'tʃeːri]

The final vowel may, of course, be given a separate note:

Lucia di Lammermoor

l'e - co de' **mie - i** la - men - ti
['lɛːko de mjɛːi laˈmenti]

Patterns of Phrasal Triphthongs

When three vowel sounds join together between words, the result is a phrasal triphthong. The most common type of phrasal triphthong involves a stress on the second of the three vowels, resulting either when a diphthong follows an unstressed final vowel:

Mor - tal, di - let - **toai** Nu - mi
[morˈtaːl diˈlɛtto‿aːi ˈnuːmi]

Aïda

Cre- do che Cassi**o ei** fosse
[ˈkreːdo ke ˈkassjo‿eːi ˈfosse]

Otello

or when the second of the three vowels is the word **a, è, e, o** (meaning *or*):

La vi - ta **è in**- fer - no
[la ˈviːta‿ɛ‿inˈfɛrno]

La Forza del Destino

A te- **la o a** se - ta ri - ca- mo in casa e (fuori)
[a ˈteːla‿o‿a ˈseːta rikaːmo‿iŋˈkaːza‿e fwɔːri]

La Bohème

dan - na - to **a** e - ter - no pian - to
[dan'naːto<u>a</u>͜e'tɛrno 'pjanto]

La Forza del Destino

Rarely, phrasal triphthongs can result from three unstressed vowels:

fior ch'io fac - **cio, ahi** - mè_____
[kiːo 'fatʃo͜ <u>ai</u>'mɛ]

La Bohème

In such cases the stressed vowel (or, in the last example, the second vowel) of the phrasal diphthong receives most of the note value, although with short note values it is difficult to define vowel distribution exactly. Even if distribution is approximately equal, the correct stress must still be brought out.

Phrasal triphthongs can also result from first-vowel syllabic diphthongs followed by an unstressed vowel. The first vowel is stressed and, if the note value allows, is lengthened:

il **mioa**-mor
[il miːo͜a'moːr]

Madama Butterfly

vo - **leaun** mu - si - ci - sta
[vo'leːa͜un muzi'tʃista]

La Bohème

It is interesting to observe that phrasal triphthongs are often set to very short note values, indicating their unstressed nature within the phrase.

Just as with phrasal diphthongs, there are times when the general guidelines for phrasal triphthongs described above need to be modified for particular musical settings. Here is a famous example:

Le Nozze di Figaro

fin - chè l'a- **ria è an**- cor bru - na
[fiŋ'ke 'laːrja‿ɛ‿aŋ'koːr]

The three vowels of the phrasal triphthong should probably be distributed equally (and smoothly!) over the eighth note. Attempting to give **è** more time can detract from the smooth transition between vowel sounds and thus the overall legato line.

This famous phrase from another famous aria is a rare (perhaps unique) example of a phrasal triphthong of three unstressed vowels set to a long note:

Orfeo ed Euridice

Che fa - rò sen- **za Eu** - ri - di - ce
[ke fa'rɔ 'sɛnːtsa‿euri'diːtʃe]

The best solution here is to lengthen the [a] artificially in order to set up the most natural pronunciation of the name "Euridice." Certainly lengthening the middle vowel does not yield a satisfactory result here.

Another famous aria has a particular setting of a phrasal triphthong:

Le Nozze di Figaro

di **mia in** - fe - li - ci - ta
[di miːa‿infelitʃi'ta]

Mozart has set **mia** on a half note tied to an eighth note. The first syllable of **infelicità** should be sung on the following eighth note. The best solution for the distribution of **mia** is probably to place [a] on the second quarter note beat, although placing it on the tied eighth note is also possible. However, many singers of this aria ignore the information in the score and place the first syllable of **infelicità** on the tied eighth note, slurring it to the next eighth note. This is an incorrect reading of Mozart's setting.

Appendix:
Guidelines for
Determining Open
and Closed *e*
and *o* in the
Stressed Syllable

Students grappling with this topic frequently ask why Italian has this characteristic of some words having open vowels and some having closed vowels. The answer lies to a large extent in the development of Italian from Latin. Classical Latin uses the long and short signs (‾ ˘) over vowels, which affect pronunciation as well as having grammatical ramifications. In general, Latin words spelled with ē or *i* became Italian words with [e]: **lex, lēgis** becomes **legge** ['ledʤe] (meaning *law*). Latin words spelled with ĕ became Italian words with [ɛ]: **lĕgo, lĕgere** becomes **leggo** ['lɛggo], **leggere** ['lɛdʤere] (meaning *read*). Latin words spelled with ō or *u* became Italian words with [o]: **curro, currere** becomes **corro** ['korro] **correre** ['korrere] (meaning *run*). Latin words spelled with ŏ became Italian words with [ɔ]: **cŏr, cŏrdis** becomes **cuore** ['kwɔːre] or **core** ['kɔːre] (meaning *heart*).

Remember that spoken Italian assumes all unstressed *e*'s and *o*'s to be closed. See the discussion of these vowels in the main text for application to singing. The patterns listed below are for the stressed syllable only. Most of these patterns are subject to a substantial number of exceptions. A reliable dictionary should always be consulted.

● Stressed *e* and *o*

<u>Stressed *e* and *o* are usually open in the following five contexts.</u> (Most examples given have stressed open syllables, a few have stressed closed syllables):

1. In the antepenultimate syllable

Some Examples with *e*

gelida ['ʤɛːlida]	**tenebro** ['tɛːnebro]	**immemore** [im'mɛːmore]
celebre ['ʧɛːlebre]	**veneto** ['vɛːneto]	**cedere** ['ʧɛːdere]
merito ['mɛːrito]	**gemito** ['ʤɛːmito]	**fremito** ['frɛːmito]
Elena ['ɛːlena]	**esule** ['ɛːzule]	**edera** ['ɛːdera]
zefiro ['dzɛːfiro]	**genere** ['ʤɛːnere]	**Venere** ['vɛːnere]
secolo ['sɛːkolo]	**medico** ['mɛːdiko]	**tenero** ['tɛːnero]

anelito [a'nɛːlito] **pettine** ['pɛttine] **essere** ['ɛssere]
perfido ['pɛrfido] **vertice** ['vɛrtiʧe] **termine** ['tɛrmine]
pergola ['pɛrgola] **pendere** ['pɛndere] **perdere** ['pɛrdere]

Some Exceptions with e

fegato ['feːgato]   **femmina** ['femmina] **Cesare** ['ʧeːzare]
cembalo ['ʧembalo] **mettere** ['mettere]   **credere** ['kreːdere]
cenere ['ʧeːnere]   **debole** ['deːbole]   **vendere** ['vendere]
vedova ['veːdova]   **vendita** ['vendita]   **semplice** ['sempliʧe]
pentola ['pentola]

Some Examples with o

mobile ['mɔːbile]   **nobile** ['nɔːbile]   **opera** ['ɔːpera]
solito ['sɔːlito]   **codice** ['kɔːdiʧe]   **comico** ['kɔːmiko]
popolo ['pɔːpolo]   **povero** ['pɔːvero]   **anonimo** [a'nɔːnimo]
docile ['dɔːʧile]   **gomito** ['gɔːmito]   **complice** ['kɔːmpliʧe]
comico ['kɔːmiko]   **comodo** ['kɔːmodo]   **ottimo** ['ɔttimo]
volgere ['vɔlʤere]   **porgere** ['pɔrʤere]

Some Exceptions with o

rondine ['rondine]   **rompere** ['rompere]   **compito** ['kompito]
giovane ['ʤoːvane]   **ordine** ['ordine]   **sorgere** ['sorʤere]

2. Immediately following another vowel-letter (usually a glide)

Some Examples with e

guerra ['gwɛrra]   **guerriero** [gwer'rjɛːro]
mansueto [man'swɛːto]   **maniera** [ma'njɛːra]
pensiero [pens'jɛːro]   **sentiero** [sen'tjɛːro]
portiere [por'tjɛːre]   **cavaliere** [caval'jɛːre]
consigliere [consi'ʎʎɛːre] **cielo** ['ʧɛːlo]
cieco ['ʧɛːko]   **miei** [mjɛːi]
dietro ['djɛːtro]   **pietra** [pjɛːtra]
lieve [ljɛːve]   **lieto** [ljɛːto]
chiesa [kjɛːza]   **ieri** ['jɛːri]
fiero ['fjɛːro]   **fieno** ['fjɛːno]
pieno [pjɛːno]   **maestro** ['maɛstro]
poeta ['poɛːta]   **Raffaele** [raffaɛːle]
quercia ['kwɛrʧa]   **aereo** ['aɛːreo]

Some Exceptions with e

questo ['kwesto]   **quello** ['kwello]
paese ['pae:ze]   **saetta** ['sae̱tta]

Some Examples with o

viola ['vjɔ:la]   **idiota** ['idjɔ:ta]   **chioma** ['kjɔ:ma]
chiodo ['kjɔ:do]   **buono** ['bwɔ:no]   **cuoca** ['kwɔ:ka]
ruota ['rwɔ:ta]   **ruolo** ['rwɔ:lo]   **puoi** ['pwɔ:i]
vuoi ['vwɔ:i]   **tuoi** ['twɔ:i]   **suoi** ['swɔ:i]
pioggia ['pjɔdʤa]   **vuoto** ['vwɔ:to]   **cuoio** ['kwɔ:jo]
tuono ['twɔ:no]   **stuolo** ['stwɔ:lo]   **suolo** ['swɔ:lo]
suono ['swɔ:no]   **cuore** ['kwɔ:ɾe]   **fuoco** ['fwɔ:ko]
fuori ['fwɔ:ri]   **muoio** ['mwɔ:jo]
                             (from **morire**)

Note: Some of these words are often seen without the glide. The vowel remains open:

core [kɔ:re]   **foco** [fɔ:ko]   **gioco** (from **giuoco**) [ʤɔ:ko]

Some Exceptions with o

giorno ['ʤorno]   **Giorgio** ['ʤorʤo]   **fiore** [fjo:ɾe]
piombo ['pjombo]   **trionfo** ['triọnfo]   **maggiore** [madʤo:ɾe]

Including all words ending in *-ione*

nazione [nattsjo:ne]   **emozione** [emottsjo:ne]
ragione [raʤo:ne]   **riunione** [riunjo:ne], etc.

3. Immediately preceding another vowel-letter

Some Examples with e

lei [lɛ:i]   **sei** [sɛ:i]   **idea** [i'dɛ:a]
reo [rɛ:o]   **trofeo** [tro'fɛ:o]   **Orfeo** [or'fɛ:o]
Romeo [ro'mɛ:o]   **ebreo** [e'brɛ:o]   **dei** (pl.of dio) [dɛ:i]

Some Exceptions with e

dei (meaning "of the") [de:i]
Also: contractions in the imperfect tense
tacea (taceva) [ta'ʧe:a]   **avea (aveva)** [a've:a]
potean (potevano) [po'te:an]

Some Examples with o

poi [pɔ:i]   **boia** [bɔ:ja]   **gioia** ['ʤɔ:ja]
noia [nɔ:ja]   **soia** [sɔ:ja]   **boa** ['bɔ:a]
eroe [e'rɔ:e]   **eroico** [e'rɔ:iko]

Some Exceptions with o

noi [no:i]   **voi** [vo:i]   **coi** (con i) [ko:i]
leone ['leo:ne]   **rasoio** [ra'zo:jo]

4. Immediately preceding a consonant followed by two vowel-letters (the first usually a glide)

Some Examples with e

serio ['sɛ:rjo]   **serie** ['sɛ:rje]   **ferie** ['fɛ:rje]
tempio ['tɛmpjo]   **miseria** [mi'zɛ:rja]   **sedia** ['sɛ:dja]
medio ['mɛ:djo]   **tedio** ['tɛ:djo]   **genio** ['ʤɛ:njo]
criterio [kri'tɛ:rjo]   **inebrio** [in'ɛ:brio]   **inezia** [in'ettsja]
ingenua [in'ʤɛ:nwa]   **tenue** ['tɛ:nwe]   **etereo** [e'tɛ:reo]
tragedia [tra 'ʤɛ:dja] **commedia** [kom'mɛ:dja]
suffix -egio: **collegio** [kol'lɛ:ʤo]   **privilegio** [privi'lɛ:ʤo]

An Exception with e

tregua ['tre:gwa]

Some Examples with o

gloria ['glɔ:rja]   **storia** ['stɔ:rja]   **memoria** [me'mɔ:rja]
vittoria [vit'tɔ:rja]   **proprio** ['prɔ:prio]   **odio** ['ɔ:djo]
elogio [el'ɔ:ʤo]   **demonio** [de'mɔ:njo]   **Antonio** [an'tɔ:njo]
ovvio ['ɔvvjo]   **ozio** ['ɔttsjo]   **marmoreo** [mar'mɔ:reo]

5. Preceding a consonant cluster beginning with s

Some Examples with e

tempesta [tem'pɛsta]   **sesto** ['sɛsto]   **resto** ['rɛsto]
presto ['prɛsto]   **rovescia** [ro'vɛʃʃa]   **testa** ['tɛsta]
festa ['fɛsta]   **mesto** ['mɛsto]   **finestra** [fi'nɛstra]
foresta [fo'rɛsta]   **gesto** ['ʤɛsto]   **destra** ['dɛstra]
orchestra [or'kɛstra]   **veste** ['vɛste]   **pesca** ['pɛska]
                                                         (meaning *peach*)

and

esco [ˈɛsko]   **esci** [ˈɛʃʃi]   **esce** [ˈɛʃʃe]   **escono** [ˈɛskono] (from **uscire**)

Some Exceptions with e

questo [ˈkwesto]   **pesce** [ˈpeʃe]   **pesto** [ˈpesto]
fresco [ˈfresko]   **esca** [ˈeska]   **cespo** [ˈtʃespo]
cesta [ˈtʃesta]   **bestia** [ˈbestja]   **tedesco** [teˈdesko]
vescovo [ˈveskovo]   **pesca** [ˈpeska] (meaning *fishing*)

Some Examples with o

nostro [ˈnɔstro]   **vostro** [ˈvɔstro]   **tosto** [ˈtɔsto]
posta [ˈpɔsta]   **costa** [ˈkɔsta]   **sosta** [ˈsɔsta]
bosco [ˈbɔsko]   **Tosca** [ˈtɔska]   **angoscia** [aŋˈgɔʃʃa]
imposta [imˈpɔsta]   **rospo** [ˈrɔspo]   **oste** [ˈɔste]
chiostro [ˈkjɔstro]   **arrosto** [arˈrɔsto]

Some Exceptions with o

posto [ˈposto]   **mostro** [ˈmostro]
fosco [ˈfosko]   **conoscere** [koˈnoʃʃere] (**conosco** [koˈnosko], etc.)

● Final Stressed e and o

Final stressed *o* is always open (and short). This occurs in verb endings, specifically first person singular, future tense, and third person singular, past historic tense:

amerò [ameˈrɔ]   **sarò** [saˈrɔ]   **avrò** [avˈrɔ]
amò [aˈmɔ]   **pensò** [penˈsɔ]   **andò** [anˈdɔ]

Monosyllables vary:

ho [ɔ] (from **avere**)   **so** [sɔ] (from **sapere**)   **lo** [lo]   **o** [o]

But final stressed *e* is usually closed (and short):

- Including all words ending in -*chè* or -*ché:* **perchè** [perˈke], **finchè** [fiŋˈke], **benchè** [beŋˈke], **fuorchè** [fworˈke]
- In all combinations with *trè:* **ventitrè** [ventiˈtre]
- In all words that have apocopated -*de:* **mercè** (mercede) [merˈtʃe], **fè** (fede) [fe]

- In third person singular, past absolute tense, -ere verbs:
  credè (or **credé**) [kre'de]
- In most monosyllables: **me, te, se, sè, le, ne, nè, re, e**

Final stressed *e* is open (and short) in a few words:

è [ɛ]	**c'è** [ʧɛ]	**v'è** [vɛ]
tè [tɛ] (meaning *tea*)	**caffè** [kaf'fɛ]	**ahimè** [aï'mɛ]
Mosè [mo'zɛ]		

● Stressed *e* and *o* in Open Syllables Other Than the Above

- *e* before *gli* is usually closed:
  egli ['eʎʎi], **veglio** ['veʎʎo], **sveglia** ['zveʎʎa]
  Important exception (open e): **meglio** ['mɛʎʎo]
- *o* before *gli* is usually open:
  foglio ['fɔʎʎo], **foglia** ['fɔʎʎa], **doglie** ['dɔʎʎe],
  voglio ['vɔʎʎo], **soglio** ['sɔʎʎo], **orgoglio** [or'gɔʎʎo]
  Exceptions (closed o):
  moglie ['moʎʎe], **germoglia** ['ʤermoʎʎa]
- *e* and *o* before *gn* are both usually closed:

legno ['leɲɲo]	**convegno** [kon'veɲɲo]
segno ['seɲɲo]	**degno** ['deɲɲo]
sdegno ['zdeɲɲo]	**ingegno** [in'ʤeɲɲo]
pegno ['peɲɲo]	**regno** ['reɲɲo]
zampogna [tsam'poɲɲa]	**sogno** ['soɲɲo]
bisogno ['bizoɲɲo]	**vergogna** [ver'goɲɲa]

● Stressed *e* and *o* in Open Syllables: Single Consonants

Preceding single consonants, stressed *e* and *o* are closed more often than not, but exceptions are numerous. It is advisable to learn the common exceptions.

Some Common Words with Open e

bene ['bɛ:ne]	**breve** ['brɛ:ve]	**prego** ['prɛ:go]
sede ['sɛ:de]	**speme** ['spɛ:me]	**treno** ['trɛ:no]
prete ['prɛ:te]	**collega** [col'lɛ:ga]	**biblioteca** [biblio'tɛ:ka]
eco ['ɛ:ko]	**ero** ['ɛ:ro] **eri** ['ɛ:ri]	**era** ['ɛ:ra] (from **essere**)

Some Common Words with Open o

oro [ˈɔːro]	**coro** [ˈkɔːro]	**moto** [ˈmɔːto]
nota [ˈnɔːta]	**cosa** [ˈkɔːza]	**sposo** [ˈspɔːzo]
sposa [ˈspɔːza]	**posa** [ˈpɔːza]	**rosa** [ˈrɔːza]
roba [ˈrɔːba]	**parola** [paˈrɔla]	**prode** [ˈprɔːde]
no [nɔ]	**ho** [ɔ](from avere)	**so** [sɔ](from **sapere**)

vo' [vɔ](from **voglio, volere**)   **poco** [ˈpɔːko] or **po'** [pɔ]

See also the list of common suffixes.

● Stressed *e* and *o* in Closed Syllables: Double Consonants

Remember that a *closed syllable* is one that ends with a consonant. Patterns of stressed *e* and *o* in closed syllables:

Stressed *e* or *o* before a double consonant is sometimes open, sometimes closed. Words must be learned individually, and a reliable dictionary is essential. Here are a few examples:

bella [ˈbɛlla]	**stella** [ˈstella]	**donna** [ˈdɔnna]	**sonno** [ˈsonno]
sesso [ˈsɛsso]	**spesso** [ˈspesso]	**cotto** [ˈkɔtto]	**rotto** [ˈrotto]
pezzo [ˈpɛttso]	**vezzo** [ˈvettso]	**coppia** [ˈkɔppja]	**doppio** [ˈdoppjo]
petto [ˈpɛtto]	**tetto** [ˈtetto]	**rocca** [ˈrɔkka]	**bocca** [ˈbokka]
ecco [ˈɛkko]	**secco** [ˈsekko]	**molle** [ˈmɔlle]	**pollo** [ˈpollo]
legge (*read*) [ˈledʤe]	**legge** (*law*) [ˈledʤe]	**nozze** [ˈnɔttse]	**pozzo** [ˈpottso]
Giuseppe [ʤuˈzɛppe]	**ceppi** [ˈʧeppi]	**rosso** [ˈrɔsso]	**tosse** [ˈtosse]

● Stressed e and o before Clusters Beginning L, M, N, R

All other closed syllables end in *l*, *m*, *n*, or *r*. When stressed *e* is followed by a cluster beginning with one of these consonants, it is usually open (excluding certain suffixes and verb endings). Clusters with stressed *-el* and *-em* are rare, those with stressed *-en* and *-er* are common.

- *stressed -el + cons*:
  Guglielmo [guˈʎʎɛlmo], **pompelmo** [pomˈpɛlmo]
- *stressed -em + cons*:
  sempre [ˈsɛmpre], **tempo** [ˈtɛmpo], **membro** [ˈmɛmbro]

- *stressed -en + cons*:

cento ['tʃɛnto]	**centro** ['tʃɛntro]	**senza** ['sɛntsa]
gente ['gɛnte]	**senso** ['sɛnso]	**lento** ['lɛnto]
attendere [at'tɛndere]		**immenso** [im'mɛnso]
difendere [di'fɛndere]		**vento** (*wind*)['vɛnto]

including common suffixes *-ento* (but not *-mento*), *-ente* (but not *-mente*), *-enza*, *-endo*:

contento [kon'tɛnto]	**argento** [ar'gɛnto]
ardente [ar'dɛnte]	**torrente** [tor'rɛnte]
presenza [pre'zɛntsa]	**partenza** [par'tɛntsa]
scrivendo [skri'vɛndo]	**bevendo** [be'vɛndo]

- *stressed -er + cons*:

aperto [a'pɛrto]	**cervo** ['tʃɛrvo]	**Berta** ['bɛrta]
serto ['sɛrto]	**servo** ['sɛrvo]	**verba** ['vɛrba]
eterno [e'tɛrno]	**verso** ['vɛrso]	**erba** ['ɛrba]
verme ['vɛrme]	**terme** ['tɛrme]	**inferno** [in'fɛrno]
terzo ['tɛrtso]	**inerme** [in'ɛrme]	**governo** [go'vɛrno]
perla ['pɛrla]	**coperto** [co'pɛrto]	**Minerva** [min'ɛrva]
concerto [kon'tʃɛrto]	**certo** ['tʃɛrto]	

Some exceptions (closed *e* before cluster beginning *l*, *m*, *n*, or *r*):

cembalo ['tʃembalo]	**cerchio** ['tʃerkjo]	**empio** ['empjo]
verde ['verde]	**Verdi** ['verdi]	**venti** (*twenty*) ['venti]
selva ['selva]	**belva** ['belva]	**entro** ['entro]
dentro ['dentro]	**pentola** ['pentola]	**vendere** ['vendere]
fermo ['fermo]	**per** [per]	suffixes *-mente, -mento*
		scherzo ['skertso]

When stressed *o* is followed by a cluster beginning with *l*, *m*, *n*, or *r* the patterns are:

- *Stressed -ol + consonant is usually closed:*

colpa ['kolpa]	**dolce** ['doltʃe]	**molto** ['molto]
volgo ['volgo]	**folto** ['folto]	**stolto** ['stolto]
golfo ['golfo]	**sepolcro** [se'polkro]	**volpe** ['volpe]
colmo ['kolmo]	**colpa** ['kolpa]	**polpa** ['polpa]
oltre ['oltre]	**polvere** ['polvere]	**volto** ['volto]
ascolto [a'skolto]	**colto** ['kolto]	(meaning
(from **ascoltare**)	(meaning	*face*)
	cultivated)	

Some exceptions (open *o*):

risolve [ri'sɔlve] **soldi** ['sɔldi] **volta** ['vɔlta] (meaning *turn*)
colta ['kɔlta] (meaning *harvest*) **tolto** ['tɔlto] (from **togliere**)
volgere ['vɔldʒere]

● *Stressed -om + consonant is usually closed:*

ombra ['ombra]   **tomba** ['tomba]   **tromba** ['tromba]
bomba ['bomba]   **piombo** ['pjombo] **colomba** [ko'lomba]
ingombro [iŋ'gombro] **rompere** ['rompere] **compito** ['kompito]

● *Stressed -on + consonant is usually closed:*

conte ['konte]   **mondo** ['mondo]   **bionda** ['bjonda]
donde ['donde]   **secondo** [se'kondo] **contro** ['kontro]
fondo ['fondo]   **fronte** ['fronte]   **fronda** ['fronda]
rondine ['rondine]   **tronco** ['troŋko]   **bronzo** ['brondzo]
con [kon]   **tondo** ['tondo]   **non** [non]

Some exceptions (open *o*): **conscio** ['kɔnʃo], **console** ['kɔnsole]

● *Stressed -or + consonant is about equally divided:*

Open:

morte ['mɔrte]   **sorte** ['sɔrte]   **forte** ['fɔrte]
forza ['fɔrtsa]   **corpo** ['kɔrpo]   **corvo** ['kɔrvo]
porta ['pɔrta]   **corda** ['kɔrda]   **torto** ['tɔrto]
morso ['mɔrso]   **scorno** ['skɔrno]   **coorte** [ko'ɔrte]
morbido ['mɔrbido]   **mordere** ['mɔrdere] **torcere** ['tɔrtʃere]
comporto [kom'pɔrto] **consorte** [kon'sɔrte] **ricordo** [ri'kɔrdo]

Closed:

bordo ['bordo]   **borgo** ['borgo]   **borsa** ['borsa]
corto ['korto]   **corsa** ['korsa]   **forse** ['forse]
forno ['forno]   **giorno** ['dʒorno]   **torta** ['torta]
sorso ['sorso]   **sordo** ['sordo]   **forma** ['forma]
orso ['orso]   **ordine** ['ordine]   **intorno** [in'torno]
dintorno [din'torno] **risorsa** [ri'sorsa] **sorgere** ['sordʒere]

The reader will have noticed that sometimes more than one of the patterns described throughout this appendix can apply to a given word. A word such as **perfido** has both an antepenult stress and a stressed -*er* pattern, both of which suggest an open *e*, which is in fact the case. Sometimes two patterns fitting a single word are at odds, and one takes precedence over the other. Thus in the word **rondine**, the stressed -*on* pattern (suggesting a closed *o*) takes precedence over the antepenult word stress. In the word **fiore** (and other -*iore* words), the -*ore* noun suffix, with closed *o*, takes precedence over the glide-vowel pattern, but in **cuore** (open *o*) the opposite is true. Very occasionally two patterns suggest the same result, but the opposite obtains: **pentola** has a closed e in spite of the antepenult stress and stressed -*en* pattern. Verb infinitives can be particularly difficult in this regard: **conoscere** has both an antepenult stress and a stressed *o* before a cluster beginning with *s*, yet the *o* is closed; **vendere** has an antepenult stress and a stressed -*en* pattern, yet the *e* is closed.

● **Suffixes**

- Common suffixes that always have stressed closed *e* before a double consonant, consonant cluster, or in the antepenultimate syllable:

  -*essa*: **contessa** [kon'tessa], **baronessa** [baro'nessa]
  -*etto*: **Rigoletto** [rigo'letto], **caminetto** [kami'netto]
  -*etta*: **Violetta** [vjo'letta], **Musetta** [mu'zetta]

  Note: when -*etto* and -*etta* are diminutive endings, as above, the e is closed. When they are *not* diminutive endings, the *e* is open:

  letto ['lɛtto] **diletto** ['lɛtto] **affetto** [af'fɛtto] **perfetto** [per'fɛtto]

  -*ezza*: **bellezza** [bel'lettsa], **fierezza** [fje'rettsa]
  -*eccia*: **freccia** ['frettʃa], **breccia** ['brettʃa]
  -*eggio*: **pareggio** [pa'reddʒo], **corteggio** ['korteddʒo]
  -*efice*: **carnefice** [kar'ne:fitʃe], **orefice** [o're:fitʃe]
  -*evole*: **piacevole** [pja'tʃe:vole], **colpevole** [kol'pe:vole]
  -*mente*: **lentamente** [lenta'mente], **dolcemente** [doltʃe'mente]

  Note: Otherwise -*ente*- has OPEN *e*. See below.

  -*mento*: **portamento** [porta'mento], **tradimento** [tradi'mento], **tormento** [tor'mento]

Note: Otherwise *-ento-* has OPEN *e*. See below.

● Common suffixes with stressed open *e*:

-ello(a): **gemello** [ʤe'mɛllo], **damigella** [dami'ʤɛlla] (but
 not **ella** ['ella] or **capello** [ka'pello])
-ente: **presente** [pre'zɛnte], **dolente** [do'lɛnte]
-ento: **contento** [kon'ɛnto], **cento** ['ʧɛnto], **lento** ['ɛnto]
-ero: **mistero** [mi'stɛːro], **impero** [im'pɛːro]
-esimo: **centesimo** [ʧen'tɛːzimo], **undicesimo** [undi'ʧɛːzimo]
-estre: **silvestre** [sil'vɛstre], **calpestre** [kal'pɛstre]
-enza: **partenza** [par'tɛntsa], **confidenza** [konfi'dɛntsa]

● Common suffixes with stressed closed o:

-ore: **dottore** [dot'toːre], **amore** [a'moːre], **fiore** ['fjoːre]
 (but **cuore** ['kwɔːre])
-one: **ragione** [ra'ʤoːne], **maledizione** [maledit'tsjoːne],
 farafallone [farafal'loːne]
-oso: **amoroso** [amo'roːzo], **pietoso** [pje'toːzo], **doloroso**
 [dolo'roːzo] (dictionaries give this suffix as [oːso])

● Common suffixes with stressed open o:

-oro: **tesoro** [te'zɔːro], **Lindoro** [lin'dɔːro], **ristoro** [ri'stɔːro],
 oro ['ɔːro]
 But not **loro** ['loːro], **coloro** [ko'loːro], **costoro**
 [ko'stoːro]
-otto: **vecchiotto** [vek'kjɔtto], **giovinotto** [ʤovi'nɔtto]
-olo(a): **figliolo** [fi'ʎʎɔːlo]

● Verb endings with stressed closed *e*:

-emmo: **avemmo** [a'vemmo], **credemmo** [kre'demmo]
 (past absolute tense), **avremmo** [a'vremmo],
 crederemmo [krede'remmo] (conditional)
-esse: **avesse** [a'vesse], **credesse** [kre'desse] (imperfect
 subjunctive),
-essi: **avessi** [a'vessi], **credessi** [kre'dessi] (imperfect
 subjunctive)
-esso(a): **messo** ['messo], **permessa** [per'messa]
 (past participle)
-esti: **avesti** [a'vesti], **credesti** [kre'desti] (past absolute),
 avresti [a'vresti], **crederesti** [krede'resti] (conditional)
-este: **aveste** [a'veste], **credeste** [kre'deste] (past absolute),
 avreste [a'vreste], **credereste** [krede'reste] (conditional)

-evano: **avevano** [a'veːvano], **credevano** [kre'deːvano]
(imperfect)

-erono: **crederono** [kre'deːɾono] (past absolute)

-essero: **avessero** [a'vesseɾo], **credessero** [kre'desseɾo]
(imperfect subjunctive)

-essimo: **avessimo** [a'vessimo], **credessimo** [kre'dessimo]
(imperfect subjunctive)

- Verb endings with stressed open e:

-ebbe: **avrebbe** [av'rɛbbe], **crederebbe** [krede'rɛbbe]
(conditional tense)

-ebbero: **avrebbero** [av'rɛbbeɾo], **crederebbero** [krede'rɛb-
beɾo] (conditional)

-endo: **avendo** [a'vɛndo], **credendo** [kre'dɛndo] (gerund)

GERMAN

Introduction

German has a reputation as a difficult language. This is true of the grammar, which is more complex than English, and results in many more word inflections. The reputation for difficulty carries over into the pronunciation of the language, which is also often described as "guttural." Mastering certain sounds that do not occur in English may present some difficulty (more so is the sequencing of certain sounds in phrases), but the relationship between spelling and pronunciation is very logical and consistent (German is nearly as phonetic as Italian, and much more so than French and English). Of the two sounds that could be considered guttural, one (the uvular pronunciation of r) is not used in singing, and the other (the *ach-Laut* [x]) is very light and of short duration.

The sound patterns of German are much closer to English than are those of Italian and French. English is, after all, a Germanic language. Once mastery of the German sounds that do not occur in English is complete, phrasal inflection tends to come more easily than for the Romance languages.

To achieve an intermediate level of proficiency with German diction the student must master the following areas:

1. An understanding of German word structure, which significantly affects the pronunciation of German, in particular vowel quality and length
2. Proper pronunciation of the *ich-Laut* [ç] and the *ach-Laut* [x] and when each is used
3. Correct and consistent formation of the mixed vowels
4. Correct and consistent formation of [e] and [o]
5. Proper sequencing and articulation of consecutive consonant sounds, within and between words

67

International Phonetic Alphabet (IPA) Symbols for German

Vowels	Plosive Consonants	Lateral Consonants
[a] [a:] **Mann, Vater**	[b] **beben**	
[e] [e:] **Melodie, Demut**	[p] **Pracht, pfeife, ab**	[l] **Licht, füllen**
[ɛ] [ɛ:] **denn, Träne**	[d] **dadurch**	
[i] [i:] **Universität,**	[t] **Teil, retten, Bad**	*Affricate Consonants*
liegen	[g] **gegen**	
[I] **bin, inmitten**	[k] **Knie, blicken, Tag**	[ts] **zehn**
[o] [o:] **woran, Sohn**		[tʃ] **Deutsch**
[ɔ] **Sonne, trocken**	*Fricative Consonants*	
[u] [u:] **Juwel, Buch**		*Vibrant Consonants*
[U] **Mutter, Ungeduld**	[v] **Wagen, Klavier**	
[y] [y:] **Psychologie,**	[f] **von, Philosoph**	[r] **rot, irren**
Bücher	[s] **essen, bis**	
[Y] **Mütter, Glück**	[ʃ] **spät, Stern, rasch**	*Other Symbols*
[ø] [ø:] **Ökonomie,**	[z] **See, gewesen**	
böse	[ç] **ich, Milch**	[:] **long vowel**
[œ] **plötzlich,**	[h] **Hoheit**	['] **syllabic stress**
mißgönnen	[x] **ach, machen**	[|] **glottal separation**
[ə] **gegeben, Liebe**		
[ɐ] **Bruder, der**	*Nasal Consonants*	
Glide	[n] **nennen**	
	[m] **mehr, immer**	
[j] **ja, jetzt, Lilie**	[ŋ] **singen, danken**	

Dictionaries and Pronunciation Reference Books

Some German/English dictionaries employ the IPA and some do not. It is recommended that the student acquire a dictionary using IPA, with the understanding that some dictionaries use a nonstandard IPA system for German vowels. While this text employs the standard IPA system that is used by Siebs and Duden (see below), the alternative system has only one IPA symbol for the open and closed vowel pairs. If the symbol has no colon it is considered the open version of the vowel; if the symbol is followed by a colon it is considered the closed version of the vowel. In this system, German **wer** would be transcribed as [ve:r] and **wenn** would be transcribed as [ven]. The more standard transcription of **wenn** is [vɛn].

The problem with the alternative approach is that there is no way to indicate those cases in which a closed vowel is short in duration, which is often the case with words of non-Germanic origin. Thus **Melodie** would be transcribed [melodi:] and one would incorrectly assume that the first two syllables have open vowels. The system used by Siebs, Duden, and most diction texts would transcribe this word the same way, but since [e] and [o] represent closed vowels only, the reader would know that all vowels in this word are closed.

The two standard reference books for German pronunciation are *Deutsche Aussprache* by Theodor Siebs and *Duden Aussprache-wörterbuch* (see Bibliography at the end of this book). They are available in German-language editions only. The Siebs book was originally published in 1898 and has since been revised and reprinted in numerous updated editions. The Duden was published in 1990 and is volume six of the Duden series of books on the German language.

Both books have the same general format, consisting of introductory sections discussing various aspects of German pronunciation followed by an alphabetical listing of German and non-German words and proper names with IPA transcriptions. While these books are written with the spoken language in mind, they are invaluable resources for the singer as well, especially for proper names and for foreign and other unusual words. There are minor differences in their respective applications of IPA, most notably diphthongs, and [a] versus [ɑ].

The Umlaut

The *Umlaut* (¨) is the only diacritical mark used in German. The word can be translated roughly as "sound modification" and refers specifically to vowels. It occurs over the vowel-letters *a*, *o*, and *u*, and the diphthong *au*, thereby changing their sounds:

- The letter *a* sounds as [a] or [a:] *but* the letter *ä* sounds as [ɛ] or [ɛ:]
- The letter *o* sounds as [ɔ] or [o:] *but* the letter *ö* sounds as [œ] or [ø:]
- The letter *u* sounds as [U] or [u:] *but* the letter *ü* sounds as [Y] or [y:]
- The diphthong *au* sounds as [ao] *but* the diphthong *äu* sounds as [ɔø]

Word Origin: Germanic and Non-Germanic

Over the centuries the German language has absorbed into its vocabulary a large number of words derived from Latin and Greek. Many such words are very common, such as **privat**, **Musik**, **Bar-**

bier. The casual student of German is not necessarily aware of this until encountering a less common word, for example **benedeit**, in which word stress and vowel quality might seem confusing. The student must be aware of these two broad categories of words, Germanic and non-Germanic, and two important points concerning them:

- Patterns of word stress are different in non-Germanic words than they are in Germanic words.
- Patterns of determining vowel quality (open or closed) and vowel length (long or short) are different in non-Germanic words than they are in Germanic words.

The specific patterns are given in the sections dealing with those topics.

Vowels and Vowel Length

Most German vowel sounds are paired, open and closed, with each sound of the pair represented by the same vowel-letter. It is helpful to organize and discuss them this way:

Vowel-Letter	Closed Sound	Open Sound	Alternative Sound
i	[i:] wider	[I] Winter	
(ie)	[i:] wieder	—	[jə] Lilie
e	[e:] sehen	[ɛ] senden	[ə] sehen
o	[o:] Dom	[ɔ] Dorn	
u	[u:] rufen	[U] runden	
ü, y	[y:] fühlen	[Y] füllen	
ö	[ø] König	[œ] können	
a	—	[a] sangen	[a:] sagen
ä	—	[ɛ] Blätter	[ɛ:] Bläser

The table gives all German single vowel-letters with the IPA representation of their possible sounds. In addition, the combination *ie* is given. All other vowel combinations are normally diphthongs, discussed on p. 92.

In words of Germanic origin, there is a consistent relationship between vowel *quality* (whether it is open or closed) and vowel *length* (whether it is long or short in duration):

- Closed vowels in the stressed syllable are always long.
- Open vowels (except [a:] and [ɛ:]) are always short.

Long vowel sounds are indicated in IPA by the colon [:] as shown in the table.

- Long vowel sounds are about twice as long as short ones, but this can be influenced by relative importance of a word within a phrase.
- Closed and long vowel sounds normally occur only in stressed syllables, but this can include secondary stresses in compound words (**Abendlied** ['a:bəntli:t]), or secondary stresses in words with separable prefixes (**anklagen** ['ankla:gən]).
- In words of non-Germanic origin, however, pretonic vowel sounds are often closed and short: **repetieren** [repe'ti:rən].
- Note that *a* and *ä* are the only vowel-letters with only one quality (open), but they may be long or short:

Stall [ʃtal] **Stahl** [ʃta:l] **Länder** ['lɛndɐ] **Läden** ['lɛ:dən]

Also, some long/closed vowels occur in German suffixes (*-los*, *-bar*, *-sal*, *-sam*), resulting in such sounds occurring in unstressed syllables: **langsam** ['laŋza:m].

Note also that the letter *e* has a third possible sound, the neutral vowel schwa [ə]. (See sections on "Word Stress" and "Guidelines for Vowel Quality" for a more detailed discussion of the situations described above.) The following pages discuss individual vowel sounds in detail.

Vowel Sounds

● **[i:], [I]**

The sound [i:] is usually spelled *ie* but can also be spelled with *i*.

When *ie* occurs in the stressed syllable it is pronounced [i:] as in the English word **seen**:

fliegen ['fli:gən] **nieder** ['ni:dɐ] **geblieben** [gə 'bli:bən]

When *ie* occurs in an unstressed syllable or is divided over two syllables, the word is of non-Germanic origin and rules of pronunciation are different. See p. 90.

If *i* is the only vowel in the stressed syllable, it will be pronounced [i:] if followed by a single consonant, as in **wider** [vi:dɐ]. A much more common pattern for [i:] is stressed *i* followed by *h*:

ihm [i:m] **ihn** [i:n] **ihnen** ['i:nən] **ihre** ['i:rə]

In words of non-Germanic origin, *i* will be pronounced closed if it is followed by only one consonant, regardless of word stress. If it is in the stressed syllable it will be long; if it is in an unstressed syllable it will be short: **Dirigent** [diri'gɛnt], **Musik** [mu'zi:k]. See p. 89.

The sound [I] is the same as the [I] of British English, but the American version is rather different. The latter tends to be wider and lower, the former higher and more pointed. Compare the word **bitter**, which is common to both languages. The American pronunciation is different from the British and German pronunciations. Compare these lists of words with [I]:

German	English
mit	mitt
ist	is
in, im	in
Bild	built
sich	sick

In German, [I] occurs in stressed syllables when *i* is followed by more than one consonant in the word stem:
finden ['fɪndən], **geblickt** [gə'blɪkt].

[I] occurs whenever *i* is the only vowel-letter in an unstressed syllable (in words of Germanic origin): **endlich** ['ɛntlɪç], **selig** ['ze:lɪç].

In singing, it is often desirable to "cheat" the sound [I] toward [i]. Particularly in longer note values the greater focus of [i] can yield a vocally more satisfying result. Caution is advised, however; this is not license to change every occurrence of [I] to [i].

● **[e:], [ɛ]**

These two sounds are spelled with the letter *e* when it is the only vowel-letter in the stressed syllable. If the *e* is doubled within the word stem (**Seele** [ze:lə]), followed by *h* (**fehlen** [fe:lən]), or followed by only one consonant in the word stem (**beten** [be:tən]), the result is [e:]. If the *e* is followed by two or more consonants in the stem it is open [ɛ]. See p. 92 for exceptions and monosyllables.

The sound [e:] does not normally exist in English, although it is approximated in certain diphthong sounds in English. Compare:

German	English
der [de:ɐ]	**dare** [deɚ]
geht [ge:t]	**gate** [geIt]
Lehm [le:m]	**lame** [leIm]
Seel' [ze:l]	**sail** [seIl]

The German sound not only has no diphthong, it is also more closed than the first sound of the English diphthongs. In fact [e:] is very close to [i:]. Virtually all problems in pronouncing this vowel involve pronouncing it with a diphthong or pronouncing it too open, close to [ɛ].

This is extremely important for singing! The vocal position for [e:] is nearly the same as, and sometimes identical to, the vocal position for [i:]. If difficulty is encountered with [e:], substitute [i:]. It will almost always sound right. See p. 128 for the same sound in French.

The sound [ɛ] does exist in English but it is slightly different from its German counterpart. The situation is identical to that with [I]. As with that vowel, the German version of [ɛ] is higher and more pointed than it is in American English. Compare:

German	English
Bett [bɛt]	**bed** [bɛd]
denn [dɛn]	**then** [ðɛn]
hell [hɛl]	**hell** [hɛl]
nett [nɛt]	**net** [nɛt]

Refer to the discussion of appropriate vocalization of this sound on p. 13.

[ɛ] can also be spelled with *ä*. See p. 74.

Some German words have double *ee* which separate into different word elements and syllables. This occurs most commonly with the prefixes *ge-* and *be-* preceding a stem beginning with *e*. The first *e* is pronounced as schwa, the second as [e] or [ɛ] initiated with a light glottal stroke, indicated by [|]: **beenden** [bə|ɛndən], **geehrt** [gə|e:rt]. Also with *be-* and *ge-* preceding *ein-*: **beeinflüssen** [bə|ʔaenflYsən], **geeinigt** [gə|ʔaenIçt].

A few words of non-Germanic origin have plural forms in [e:ən]. There is no glottal separation:

Fee [fe:] **Feen** ['fe:ən] **Museum** [mu'ze:Um] **Museen** [mu'ze:ən]

● [ə]

This sound is spelled only with the letter *e* in unstressed syllables.

The sound [ə] is called "schwa." It is a special case. The symbol [ə] represents a short, unstressed neutral vowel sound. The actual nature of the sound varies from language to language. Compare the versions of schwa in English, French, and German:

- pretonic: **again** [ə'gɛn], **fenêtre** [fənɛtr(ə)], **geliebt** [gə'li:pt]
- posttonic: **fireman** ['faɚmən], **livre** [livr(ə)], **Liebe** ['li:bə]

When the schwa is artificially lengthened, as it regularly is in singing, it is effectively no longer schwa, since by definition schwa is short and neutral. One must therefore determine an appropriate vowel sound to sustain. (See discussion of French schwa on p. 135.)

In German, the sound to sustain is essentially [ɛ], with the understanding that it is *unstressed* (therefore unemphasized) and can subtly change color (slightly more closed or more open) according to context.

There are two common ways in which English-speaking singers sound unidiomatic with German schwa. One is to overly round the lips and sound too French. The other is to pronounce it much too open and far back, as in English. Thus **Liebe** ['liːbə] becomes ['liːbʌ] ("lee-buh"). German schwa must maintain the height of [ɛ] but remain unstressed.

Although the sound of German schwa is as described above, it is still desirable to use the symbol [ə] when using IPA. Most dictionaries and texts use this symbol. It is also helpful in differentiating when *e* is stressed and when it is unstressed.

With the exception of words of non-Germanic origin (see p. 89); the prefixes *er-*, *ver-*, *zer-*, *ent-*, and *emp-*; and the isolated word **lebendig**, all unstressed *e*'s are to be transcribed as [ə]. Often there is more than one in a word:

eine ['aenə]   **vielen** ['fiːlən]
manches ['manʃəs]   **beenden** [bə'ɛndən]
gegebenen [gə'geːbənən]   **folgenden** ['fɔlgəndən]
Gelegenheit [gə'leːgənhaet]
Wanderer ['vandərər] or ['vandərɐ] (see p. 97 concerning *r*)

● **[ɛ], [ɛː] (spelled ä)**

The letter *ä* will result in one of these two sounds, the only difference being one of length. If the *ä* is followed by *h* (**wähnen** ['vɛːnən]) or by one consonant in the word stem (**Väter** ['fɛːtɐ]), it will be long [ɛː]. If it is followed by two consonants in the stem (**Blätter** ['blɛtɐ]), it will be short [ɛ]. The vowel quality is the same as discussed under [ɛ] on p. 73.

Some German speakers pronounce [ɛː] in a more closed fashion, near to or identical with [eː]. Some commentators describe this sound as somewhere between [ɛː] and [eː]. This text will follow the example of Siebs and Duden and use [ɛː] for the long version of this vowel, while again acknowledging that the IPA is an imperfect tool and urging students to become sensitive to subtle shadings of vowel sounds as they become more familiar with the language.

Compare vowel sounds and lengths in these words:

[ɛ:] spelled ä	**[ɛ] spelled ä**	**[ɛ] spelled e**
Väter ['fɛːtɐ]	**Blätter** ['blɛtɐ]	**Vetter** ['fɛtɐ]
Tränen ['trɛːnən]	**trällern** ['trɛlɐn]	**trennen** ['trɛnən]
fährt [fɛːrt]	**fälschen** ['fɛlʃən]	**Ferse** ['fɛrzə]
nächst [nɛːçst]	**Nächte** ['nɛçtə]	**necken** ['nɛkən]

In singing, vowel length is largely predetermined by the composer in the note values chosen for each word. Nevertheless, the singer must learn sensitivity to vowel length for those styles of singing that would require it more, such as recitative or parlando.

● **[o:], [ɔ]**

These two sounds are spelled only with the letter *o*. In the stressed syllable, if the *o* is doubled (**Boot** [boːt]) or is immediately followed by *h* (**wohnen** ('voːnən]) or by only one consonant in the word stem (**loben** ['loːbən]), it will be closed [oː]. If it is followed by two consonants in the word stem (**wollen** ['vɔlən]), it will be open [ɔ]. See p. 88 for unstressed *o*.

The sound [oː] is analogous to [eː] in that the nearest equivalent in English is always part of a diphthong. Compare:

German	**English**
Lohn [loːn]	**loan** [loUn]
Boot [boːt]	**boat** [boUt]
Not [noːt]	**note** [noUt]
vor [foːr]	**for** [foɚ]
Kohl [koːl]	**coal** [koUl]

Just as [eː] is close to [iː], so [oː] is close to [uː]. Whenever a singer has difficulty identifying the position of [oː] it is helpful to sing [uː].

The sound [ɔ] does have a counterpart in English, although it is not usually spelled with the letter *o*. Moreover, British and American English often use this sound in different words:

German	**British**	**American**
Topf	top	taught
noch	not	nought
Stock	stock	stalk
von	fog	fawn
offen	often	often

Note that the German sound is consistently short (the English sounds vary in length) and is shaped with a high point. Such height is sometimes true of British English, almost never true of standard American English.

Since the letter *o* when stressed is often pronounced [a] in American English (e.g., **not** [nat]), the American singer must be careful not to open the sound too far. The vowel of **noch** [nɔx] is different from that of **nach** [naːx].

● **[uː], [U]**

These two sounds are spelled only with the letter *u*. In the stressed syllable the *u* is closed when followed by *h* (**Ruhm** [ruːm]) or only one consonant in the stem (**Tugend** ['tuːgənt]). The letter *u* is not doubled within a word stem. If the *u* is followed by two or more consonants in the stem it will be open (**Mutter** ['mUtɐ]. See p. 89 for unstressed *u*.

The sound [uː] is equivalent in English and German. English speakers, however, often do not pronounce this sound in a pure form, but end it with a diphthong glide-off caused by the lips moving further forward while sustaining the [uː]. One often hears tongue tension in this vowel as well, which causes something like the sound [y]. Such problems with this vowel are distressingly common and they tend to carry over into other languages. It is crucial to identify the correct tongue position for this vowel, and end it with no movement of the tongue or lips.

German	English
zu [tsuː]	**to** [tu]
Ruh' [ruː]	**rue** [ru]
Mut [muːt]	**moot** [mut]
Flut [fluːt]	**flute** [flut]
Schuh' [ʃuː]	**shoe** [ʃu]

The sound [U] is also equivalent in German and English. The spelling of this sound in English is usually *oo*, sometimes *u*. The tongue position is the same as for [uː] (arched toward the pharynx) but with the mouth more open.

German	English
Busch [bUʃ]	**bush** [bUʃ]
Putz [pUts]	**puts** [pUts]
Bucht [bUxt]	**book** [bUk]
Lust [lUst]	**look** [lUk]
Fluss [flUs]	**foot** [fUt]

It was mentioned under [I] that it is often desirable to "cheat" that sound toward its closed counterpart [i]. The same is true for [U]. It is common to hear good singers focus this sound in the direction of [u] to allow the sound to "sit" better vocally, especially on sustained notes. Once again, caution is urged. Not every [U] should be sung as [u].

Very rarely is the spelling -*uu*- found in German. The two vowels fall into different word elements: **Genugtuung** [gə'nu:ktu:Uŋ]. This word (which means *satisfaction*) is formed from the words **genug** and **tun**, and the suffix -*ung*.

● **[y:]**

This sound is spelled with the letter *ü*. In words of non-Germanic (Greek) origin the sound can also be spelled with the letter *y* (**Lyrik** ['ly:rIk]). If the *ü* is followed by *h* (**fühlen** ['fy:lən]) or by a single consonant in the stem (**Blüte** ['bly:tə]), the sound will be [y:]. If the *u* is followed by more than one consonant in the stem, the result is [Y] as in **füllen** ['fYlən] (see next section).

The sound [y:] is one of the four "mixed" vowel sounds in German. These sounds do not exist in standard English. A mixed vowel is one that combines elements of two other "pure" vowels. The first and more important element is the "inside" or tongue position, and the second is the "outside" or lip position.

The tongue position for [y:] is that of [i:]. The lip position is that of [u:]. One always starts with the tongue position. If difficulty is encountered in pronouncing a mixed vowel, reduce it to the tongue position only. It is the core of the sound. The lip position simply colors this core. For practice, one can say the following English words, then, keeping the vowel from the English word, shape the lips to [u:] and say the German word:

English	German
fear [fiɚ]	**für** [fy:ɐ] or [fy:r]
mead [mi:d]	**müde** ['my:də]
tear [tiɚ]	**Tür** [ty:ɐ] or [ty:r]
cease [sis]	**süss** [zy:s]
bleat [blit]	**Blüte** ['bly:tə]

A common problem is that the proper tongue position of [i:] is abandoned as the lips move to [u:] so the singer ends up with essentially [u:].

It is true that some English-speaking singers tend to always sing [i:] for [y:]. This is sheer laziness and ought to be easily corrected.

Examples of German words (all of Greek origin) in which this sound is spelled with the letter y are:

Lyrik ['lyːrɪk]   **lyrisch** ['lyːrɪʃ]   **typisch** ['tyːpɪʃ]   **Elysium** [e'lyːziŬm]

● **[Y]**

This sound results when *ü* or *y* is followed by two or more consonants in the word stem.

The sound [Y] is a mixed vowel with the tongue position of [I] and the lip position of [U]. It differs from [yː] in that the mouth (jaw) is more open. Because it is so short in duration it is a difficult sound to make in isolation. Practice:

müssen [mYsən]   **fünf** [fYnf]   **Hülle** [hYlə]   **Glück** [glYk]   **Stück** [ʃtYk]

Now compare the sounds of [yː] and [Y] and then compare them with the similar English sounds of [iː] and [I]:

German [yː]	English [iː]	German [Y]	English [I]
fühlen ['fyːlən]	**feel** [fiːl]	**füllen** ['fYlən]	**fill** [fIl]
hüte ['hyːtə]	**heat** [hiːt]	**Hütte** ['hYtə]	**hit** [hIt]
Düne ['dyːnə]	**dean** [diːn]	**dünn** [dYn]	**din** [dIn]
grün [gryːn]	**green** [griːn]	**Gründe** ['grYndə]	**grin** [grIn]

● **[ø], [œ]**

These two sounds are the remaining mixed vowel sounds and they are spelled with the letter *ö*. If this letter is followed by *h* (**Söhne** ['zøːnə]) or only one consonant in the stem (**Töne** ['tøːnə]), the sound will be [ø]. If it is followed by two or more consonants in the stem, the sound will be [œ]. See p. 91 for exceptions.

The sound [ø] is a mixed vowel formed with the tongue position of [eː] and the lip position of [oː]. It is the same sound as French **peu, feu, deux**, except that the German sound is normally long. Make sure that the core of the sound is [eː] and that the shaping of the lips to [oː] simply completes the sound. English near-equivalents are less helpful with this sound, so none is given here. Practice:

böse ['bøːzə]   **fröhlich** ['frøːlɪç]   **gewöhnlich** [gə'vøːnlɪç]
schön [ʃøːn]   **Flöte** ['fløːtə]   **trösten** ['trøːstən] (irregular)

Sometimes Americans will pronounce this vowel sound as if it contained an American retroflex *r* sound [ɝ] as in **purple**. The American sound involves tensing the tongue by pulling it back and down. There is no such tongue tension in [ø:]

The sound [œ] is a mixed vowel formed with the tongue position of [ɛ] and the lip position of [ɔ]. It is the same as French **coeur**, **fleur**, except that the German sound is always short. The mouth (jaw) position opens from [ø] and the lips are less rounded.

Hölle ['hœlə]	**köstlich** ['kœstlIç]	**Götter** ['gœtɐ]
		or ['gœtər]
völlig ['fœlIç]	**plötzlich** ['plœtslIç]	**können** ['kœnən]

The following summary should be helpful in remembering how the mixed vowels are formed. The student must not confuse these sounds:

[y:]	tongue (inside) positioned for [i:]
	lips (outside) positioned for [u:]
[Y]	tongue (inside) positioned for [I]
	lips (outside positioned for [U]
[ø:]	tongue (inside) positioned for [e:]
	lips (outside) positioned for [o:]
[œ]	tongue (inside) positioned for [ɛ]
	lips (outside) positioned for [ɔ]

The tongue position of the mixed vowel is more important. If the student has difficulty speaking or singing any mixed vowel, he or she should start with the tongue position of the vowel.

● [a], [a:]

These two sounds are spelled with the letter a. The only difference between them is one of length. If *a* is doubled (**Saal** [za:l]) or is followed by *h* (**wahr** [va:r]) or a single consonant in the stem (**sagen** ['za:gən]), the sound is long [a:]. If *a* is followed by two or more consonants in the stem (**wallen** ['valən]), the sound is short (there are some exceptions; see below). (See also the preface for a discussion of the IPA symbols [a] and [ɑ].)

The bright sound represented by [a] occurs in American English, but it is usually *not* spelled by the letter *a*. It is usually spelled by the letter *o* as in **hot, on, costume**, as pronounced by most Americans (some Americans pronounce these words with [ɑ]; British English pronounces these words with [ɔ]).

The typical problem with Americans pronouncing [a] is that it is not bright enough. It often sounds like [ɔ]. Key words to remember in this regard are German **all** [al], **alle** [alə], and American English **all** [ɔl]. The vowels are not the same!

Furthermore, English unstressed *a* is usually neutralized to schwa. Other than the suffixes *-bar*, *-sal* and *-sam* and combinations with *all-* and *da-*, unstressed a is uncommon in German, but when it occurs it remains bright [a]. (See also p. 88.) Compare:

English	**German**
alone [əˈloUn]	**allein** [aˈlaen]
balsam [ˈbɔlsəm]	**Balsam** [ˈbalzaːm]
Judas [ˈʤudəs]	**Judas** [ˈjuːdas]
Atlas [ˈætləs]	**Atlas** [ˈatlas]

In a few proper names, double *aa* divides into two syllables. The second *a* is initiated with a light glottal stroke: **Kanaan** [ˈkaːna|an], **Jochanaan** [joˈxaːna|an].

Compare long and short sounds in the following words. [aː] is about twice as long as [a]:

[aː]	**[a]**
Staat [ʃtaːt]	**Stadt** [ʃtat]
ahnen [ˈaːnən]	**ander** [ˈandɐ]
aber [ˈaːbɐ]	**ab** [ap]
Bad [baːt]	**Band** [bant]
Wagen [ˈvaːgən]	**Wange** [ˈvaŋə]

In some words, *a* plus two or more consonants is long [aː] (see list on p. 92):

- Some words with *-ach-*:
  nach [naːx], **Sprache** [ˈʃpraːxə], **Schmach** [ʃmaːx]
- Words with *-ar-* + consonant):
  Art [aːrt], **Arzt** [aːrtst], **zart** [tsaːrt]
- Isolated words:
  Bratsche [ˈbraːtʃə], **Jagd** [jaːkt], **Magd** [maːkt],
  Papst [paːpst], **Adler** [aːdlɐ]

Word Structure

In discussing Italian and French, syllabification is emphasized as an important factor in understanding pronunciation. For understanding German pronunciation, particularly vowel quality, syllabification is much less important than word structure; the two often do not coincide.

● Word Stem

The preceding discussion of German vowel sounds repeatedly referred to *word stem*. German word structure is based on *word stems* or *root stems*. The stem of a word is that part to which prefixes, suffixes, and verb endings are added. *The number of consonants ending the stem determines the quality and length of the vowel in the stem.* (Foreign-derived words, particularly the many German words derived from Latin and Greek, do not follow this pattern.)

In German, **leb** is the common stem of **leben, lebend, lebst, gelebt, lebendig, lebhaft**. Because the stem ends with just one consonant, the vowel of the stem is closed and long [e:].

In the words **retten, rettest, gerettet, Rettung, Retter**, the common stem is **rett**. Because the stem ends with two consonants, the vowel of the stem is open and short [ɛ].

Usually the stem is one syllable, but it can be polysyllabic, as in **König, Königin, Königreich**. Since the first syllable of the stem is normally stressed (see below) in a polysyllabic stem, the quality and length of the stressed vowel are determined by the number of consonants following it within the stem (the words above have [ø:]). Vowel quality for unstressed vowels within the stem follow the guidelines for unstressed vowels given on p. 87.

German irregular verbs (so-called *strong verbs*) change vowels in different forms of the verb. Sometimes the vowel quality and quantity will change with the vowel change, sometimes not. Often the spelling will make matters clear, but not always. One can learn to recognize patterns to help in remembering correct vowel color. Here are some common examples:

Long (Closed) Becomes Short (Open)	Short (Open) Becomes Long (Closed)
schliessen [i:], **schloss, geschlossen** [ɔ]	**bitten** [I], **bat** [a:], **gebeten** [e:]
giessen [i:], **goss, gegossen** [ɔ]	**kommen** [ɔ], **kam** [a:], **gekommen** [ɔ]
fliessen [i:], **floss, geflossen** [ɔ]	**treffen** [ɛ], **traf** [a:], **getroffen** [ɔ]
mögen [ø:], **mag** [a:], **mochte, gemocht** [ɔ]	**sitzen** [I], **sass** [a:], **gesessen** [ɛ]
stehen [e:], **stand, gestanden** [a]	**sprechen** [ɛ], **sprach** [a:], **gesprochen** [ɔ]
gehen [e:], **ging** [I], **gegangen** [a]	**lassen** [a], **liess** [i:], **gelassen** [a]
werden [e:], **wird** [I], **wurde** [U], **geworden** [ɔ]	**fallen** [a], **fiel** [i:], **gefallen** [a]

Vowel Changes But Length Remains Constant

rufen [u:], **rief** [i:]   **raten** [a:], **riet** [i:]
schlafen [a:], **schlief** [i:]   **tragen** [a:], **trug** [u:]
schlagen [a:], **schlug** [u:]   **geben** [e:], **gibt, gibst** [i:], **gab** [a:]
wiegen [i:], **wog** [o:]   **ziehen** [i:], **zog** [o:]

● Word Stress

Understanding word stress in German is also crucial to understanding vowel quality and length. The principal stress of a word usually falls on the first syllable of the stem: **Lieb**e, ge**liebt**, **Lieb**ling. There are occasional exceptions: For**ell**e, Zi**geun**er, le**ben**dig; words ending in -*ei* such as Brauer**ei**, Maler**ei**, Sklaver**ei** and numerous proper names such as Jo**hann**es; and especially place names: Ber**lin**, Han**no**ver, Bremer**hav**en.

German is full of compound words, which means that two or more stems are involved. The primary stress falls on the first syllable of the first stem, with secondary stresses following on the subsequent stems:

'**Mond**es*licht*   '**lieb**es*trunk*ene   '**A**bendemp*find*ung.

A consistent exception to the above rules for word stress applies to compound adverbs and similarly constructed words. They take the stress on the second element:

zu**rück**	hin**weg**	her**aus**
vor**über**	wor**auf**	all**ein**
war**um**	zu**sam**men	aller**dings**
über**haupt**	unter**wegs**	so**gar**
ein**an**der		

Word Stress in Words of Non-Germanic Origin

The German language is full of words derived from Latin and Greek. Word stress in such words generally does not conform to the patterns described on the previous page. Perhaps the most common pattern in these words finds the stress on the final syllable:

Two-syllable Words

Mu**sik**	Ak**kord**	Te**nor**
So**pran**	Kri**tik**	Fi**gur**
Per**son**	Na**tion**	Che**mie**

Three or More Syllables

Melo**die**	Kompo**nist**	interess**ant**
Psycholo**gie**	Universi**tät**	Tele**fon**

One can learn to recognize certain suffixes (*-tion, -tät, -ist*) as following this pattern.

Some words of this type end in unstressed *e* or *e* plus a consonant. The word stress falls on the preceding syllable:

Inte**res**se   Ar**ti**kel   Ana**ly**se

Many Latin- and Greek-derived words not ending in unstressed *e*, however, particularly two-syllable words, take the stress on the penult:

Amor   **Chi**na   **pur**pur   **Ly**rik   **Tech**nik   **Ba**sis

Prefixes and Word Stress

Many German words involve prefixes. Certain prefixes such as *in-* and *un-* are generally stressed (**In**haber, **In**begriff, **In**brust, **Un**glück, **Un**fall, **un**gern, **un**erhört) though there are exceptions, and some words can vary according to the sense the speaker wishes to convey.

An important aspect of German involves prefixes in verbs. Such prefixes are either *separable* or *inseparable*. Separable prefixes (derived from prepositions) are stressed in the infinitive (**an**kommen, **ein**treten), in the past participle (**an**gekommen, **ein**getreten), and in other words derived from the verb (**An**kunft, **Ein**tritt). The prefix remains stressed in the phrase when separated from the verb: ich komme **an**, sie treten **ein**.

German Verbal Separable Prefixes

ab-	**abkommen** ['apkɔmən]
an-	**anregen** ['anre:gən]
auf-	**aufmachen** ['aofmaxən]
aus-	**ausdrücken** ['aosdrYkən]
bei-	**beistehen** ['baeʃte:ən]
da-	(usually as part of compound prefix)
	davonkommen [da'fɔnkɔmən]
	dazwischentreten [da'tsvIʃəntre:tən]

German Verbal Separable Prefixes (Continued)

dar-	**darstellen**	['darʃtɛlən]
durch-	**durchbringen**	['dUrçbrIŋən]
ein-	**einreden**	['aenre:dən]
empor-	**emporragen**	[ɛm'po:ɐragən]
entgegen-	**entgegenhalten**	[ɛnt'ge:gənhaltən]
fort-	**fortsetzen**	['fɔrtzɛtsən]
heim-	**heimkehren**	['haemke:rən]
her-	**herkommen**	['he:ɐkɔmən]
hin-	**hinsehen**	[hInze:ən]
los-	**losgeben**	['lo:sge:bən]
mit-	**mitmachen**	['mItmaxən]
nach-	**nachschlagen**	['na:xʃla:gən]
nieder-	**niederlegen**	['ni:dɐle:gən]
um-	**umkehren**	['Umke:rən]
vor-	**vorsingen**	['fo:ɐzIŋən]
weg-	**wegwerfen**	['vɛkvɛɐfən]
weiter-	**weiterbringen**	['vaetɐbrIŋən]
zu-	**zugreifen**	['tsu:graefən]
zurück-	**zurückdenken**	[tsu'rYkdɛŋkən]
zusammen-	**zusammenfassen**	[tsu'zamənfasən]

Inseparable prefixes always remain attached to the stem and never take the primary stress. The most common inseparable prefixes are:

ge- [gə]	*be-* [bə]	*emp-* [ɛmp]	*ent-* [ɛnt]
er- [ɛr] or [ɛɐ]	*ver-* [fɛr], [fɛɐ]	*zer-* [tsɛr], [tsɛɐ]	

Although prepositions as prefixes are usually separable, as in the table above, sometimes they can become inseparable verbal prefixes, most commonly *unter* and *über*. They too remain attached to the stem and generally do not take the primary stress; however, nouns derived from such verbs sometimes take the stress on the prefix, sometimes not:

unter**rich**ten	ich unter**rich**te	unter**rich**tet	**Unter**richt
unter**brech**en	ich unter**breche**	unter**broch**en	Unter**brech**ung
über**trag**en	ich über**trage**	über**trag**en	**Über**trag
über**leg**en	ich über**lege**	über**legt**	Über**leg**ung

Vowels—Closed or Open? Guidelines for Determining Vowel Quality

● **Words of Germanic Origin**

Vowels in Stressed Syllables

In general, if the stressed vowel is followed by two or more consonants *that are part of the stem*, the vowel will be open and short. If the stressed vowel is doubled, followed by *h*, or followed by only one consonant in the stem, the vowel will be closed and long. Compare the stressed vowel sounds in these words:

Stressed Vowel Open	Stressed Vowel Closed
Sonne	Sohne
rupfen	rufen
Schulter	Schule
Hölle	Höhle
füllen	fühlen
innen	ihnen
senden	sehnen

Remember to identify endings. They play no role in determining the quality of the vowel in the stem: **leben, leb/st; Bote, Bot/schaft.** In compound words and verbs with separable prefixes, the vowels in the components retain their original quality: **emporgehoben** [ɛm'poːɐ̯gəhoːbən].

It is imperative to learn the common verbal endings, and the common noun/adjective suffixes that can cause a long, closed vowel to be followed by several consonants.

Verbal Endings

Present Tense		Simple Past Tense		Past Participle
ich höre	wir hören	ich hörte	wir hörten	gehört
du hörst	ihr hört	du hörtest	ihr hörtet	
er hört	sie hören	er hörte	sie hörten	

In all of these forms of the verb **hören** the stressed vowel is long and closed [øː].

Noun Suffixes

-chen (**Mädchen, Liebchen**)   *-ling* (**Frühling, Fremdling**)
-heit (**Schönheit, Eitelkeit**)   *-sal* (**Schicksal, Labsal**)
-keit (**Dankbarkeit, Sicherheit**)   *-schaft* (**Botschaft, Leidenschaft**)
-in (**Gräfin, Freundin**)   *-tum* (**Eigentum, Reichtum**)
-lein (**Blümlein, Fräulein**)   *-ung* (**Regung, Genugtuung**)
-nis (**Ergebnis, Bedürfnis**)
-ei (**Konditorei, Lorelei**) (Stress on final syllable in these words; vowels follow non-Germanic patterns.)

Adjective Suffixes

Determine the vowel quality and length in the stressed syllable of the sample nouns and adjectives given below.

-artig as in **eigenartig**
-bar as in **dankbar, sonderbar**
-haft as in **lebhaft, boshaft**
-ig as in **selig, wonnig**
-isch as in **komisch, irdisch**
-lich as in **wunderlich, vergeblich**
-sam as in **langsam, genugsam**

Monosyllabic words are subject to exceptions from the one consonant, two consonant patterns. See word lists on p. 90. For *a* and *ä* the above guidelines hold true, except that they only affect vowel length.

A stressed vowel followed by *-gn* will be closed (long) because such words were originally spelled with *-gen*:

regnen ['re:gnən] ("regenen" from **Regen**)
segnen ['ze:gnən] ("segenen" from **Segen**)
Lügner ['ly:gnɐ] ("Lügener" from **lügen**)
Wagner ['va:gnɐ] ("Wagener" from **Wagen**)

● ch and ss, ß

Stressed vowels before these combinations are sometimes open, sometimes closed.

Before *-ch*:

● *i*, *e*, and *o* are open:

ich [Iç]   **dich** [dIç]   **sich** [zIç]   **sprechen** ['ʃprɛçən]
Pech [pɛç]   **noch** [nɔx]   **doch** [dɔx]

(Exception: **hoch** [ho:x] has [o:], but **Hochzeit** [hɔxtsaet] has [ɔ].)

- *a* is sometimes long, sometimes short:

  nach [na:x]   **Sprache** ['ʃpra:xə]   **Dach** [dax]   **Bach** [bax]

- *u* and *ü* are usually closed:

  Buch [bu:x]   **Bücher** ['by:çɐ]   **Fluch** [flu:x]
  suchen ['su:xən]   **gesucht** [gə'zu:xt]

- But if the -*ch* is followed by another consonant *in the stem*, the *u* or *ü* will be open:

  Bucht [bUxt]   **Flüchtling** ['flYçtlIŋ]   **Sucht** [zUxt]

Before -*ss* and -*ß:*

- *i* and *e* are open:

  Kisse ['kIsə]   **Gebiß** [gə'bIs]   **essen** ['ɛsən]   **vergessen** [fɛr'gɛsən]

- *a* is usually short, sometimes long:

  blaß [blas]   **fassen** ['fasən]   **Maß** [ma:s]

- *o, ö, u, ü* are sometimes open, sometimes closed:

  gross [gro:s]   **Schloss** [ʃlɔs]   **grösste** ['grø:stə]
  Schlösser ['ʃlœsɐ]   **Fuß** [fu:s]   **Kuß** [kUs]
  süß [zy:s]   **küssen** ['kYsən]

(Note: ß is an amalgamation of the letters *s* and *z* from older German spelling. It has recently been officially eliminated from German usage (replaced by -*ss*-), but it will still be encountered in material printed before the ban. ß and *ss* are interchangeable except that ß cannot occur between vowels if the preceding vowel is short. Thus **Kuß** and **Kuss** are both acceptable spellings, but the plural can only be spelled **Küsse**, and the verb can only be spelled **küssen**. The plural of **Fuß** (or **Fuss**) can be spelled either **Füße** or **Füsse**.)

● **Vowels in Unstressed Syllables**

Unstressed prefixes formed from monosyllabic prepositions retain the original vowel quality, and are short because unstressed:

zu—zurück [tsuˈrYk]   **vor—vorbei** [forˈbae]   **in—inoffiziel** [Inɔfiˈtsjɛl]

In words of Germanic origin only the five "pure" vowel-letters are found in unstressed syllables (with rare exceptions). Determine vowel quality as follows.

a

Unstressed *a* is found in the suffixes *-sal, -sam, -at, -bar*. Surprisingly, the sound is LONG [a:]:

Schicksal ['ʃɪkza:l]   **Labsal** ['lapza:l]   **Heimat** ['haema:t]
Heirat ['haera:t]   **langsam** ['laŋza:m]
verwendbar [fɛɐ'vɛntba:r] (but **Monat** ['mo:nat])

It is also found in compounds with *all-* and *da-*. The a is short: **allein** [a'laen], **danach** [dana:x].

e

Unstressed *e* is almost always schwa [ə]: **gegeben** [gə'ge:bən]. Exceptions are the five prefixes *er-, ver-, zer-, emp-, ent-* (*e* followed by a consonant within the prefix), which all have [ɛ]:

erfahren [ɛɐ'fa:rən]   **vergessen** [fɛɐ'gɛsən]
zerstören [tsɛɐ'ʃtø:rən]   **empfehlen** [ɛmp'fe:lən]
entscheiden [ɛnt'ʃaedən]

The prefix *her-* when stressed or standing alone has [e:]: **herstellen** ['he:ɐʃtɛlən], **Herkunft** ['he:ɐkUnft], **hin und her** [hɪn Unt' he:ɐ]; but unstressed has [ɛ]: **heran** [hɛ'ran], **herunter** [hɛ'rUntɐ], **herbei** [hɛɐ'bae]. The adjective **lebendig** [le'bɛndɪç] is irregular.

i

Unstressed *i* is found in prefixes and suffixes and is always open:

inmitten [ɪn'mɪtən]   **Erlaubnis** [ɛɐ'laopnɪs]   **heilig** ['haelɪç]
endlich ['ɛntlɪç]   **Göttin** ['gœtɪn]   **tückisch** ['tYkɪʃ]

o

Unstressed *o* is usually closed:

- The suffix *-los* (also long):
  rastlos ['rastlo:s], **endlos** ['ɛntlo:s], **hoffnungslos** ['hɔfnUŋslo:s]
- Final *-o* (short):

desto ['dɛsto]   **Tamino** [ta'mi:no]   **Sarastro** [za'rastro]
Papageno [papa'ge:no]   **Fidelio** [fi'de:ljo]

including proper names ending in -*ow* (the *w* is silent): **von Bülow** ['by:lo]
- Final unstressed -*or* (long) (according to Duden; Siebs has open and short!): **Doktor** ['dɔkto:r], **Marmor** ['marmo:r]
- Isolated words (note length): **Forelle** [fo'rɛlə], **Kleinod** ['klaeno:t], **Herzog** ['hɛrtso:k]
- The word **Bischof** ['bɪʃɔf] (open, short)

u

Unstressed *u* is closed in the suffixes -*mut* and -*tum*:

Demut ['de:mu:t]   **Armut** ['armu:t]   **Heiligtum** ['haelɪçtu:m]

It is OPEN in the prefix *un*- and the suffix -*ung*:

unruhig ['Unru:Iç]   **Unglück** ['UnglYk]
Stellung ['ʃtɛlUŋ]   **Prüfung** ['pry:fUŋ]

● Words of Non-Germanic Origin

As noted on p. 69, German is full of words derived from Latin and Greek. Just as *word stress* patterns in such words are different from those in words of Germanic origin, so are the rules for determining *vowel quality*.

Because such words do not usually involve word stems, pretonic vowels (that is, vowels in syllables preceding the word stress) and tonic vowels (those in the stressed syllable) normally determine their quality simply by how many consonants follow:

- If only one consonant follows a vowel in a pretonic syllable, the vowel is closed: **renovieren** [reno'vi:rən]
- If in a pretonic syllable two or more consonants follow, the vowel is usually open: **effektiv** [ɛfɛk'ti:f].

Vowel *length* follows the pattern that pretonic vowels are always short (even when closed as in **Musik** [mu'zi:k) and tonic vowels are short if open, long if closed.

Dirigent [diri'gɛnt]   **Telefon** [tele'fo:n]
Psychologie [psyçolo'gi:]   **intensiv** [Intɛn'zi:f]
Orchester [ɔr'kɛstɐ]   **Partitur** [parti'tu:r]
Katastrophe [kata'stro:fə] (*ph* considered one consonant = f)
Requisit [rekvi'zi:t]   **rekreieren** [rekre'i:rən]
(the Latin prefix *re*- always has closed [e] in German words)

Although the open sound [ɛ:] is long:
ordinär [ɔrdi'nɛ:r], **Universität** [univɛrzi'tɛ:t].

Posttonic vowels are open if followed by a consonant, closed if final. They are always short:

Lyrik ['ly:rɪk]   **purpur** ['pUrpUr]   **Fidelio** [fi'de:ljo]   **Alibi** ['alibi]

Posttonic *e* is usually schwa: **Interesse** [Inte'rɛsə], **Artikel** [ar'ti:kəl]; but occasionally not: **Sokrates** ['zo:kratɛs].

There is a family of words that ends in unstressed *-ie* or *-ien*, pronounced [jə] and [jən]:

Familie [fa'mi:ljə]   **Lilie** ['li:ljə]   **Tragödie** [tra'gø:djə]
Komödie [ko'mø:djə]   **Italien** [i'ta:ljən]   **Spanien** ['ʃpa:njən]
(but **Italiener** [ital'je:nɐ] **Spanier** ['ʃpa:njɐ])

Words ending in *stressed -ie* (pronounced [i:]) take a plural of *-ien* (pronounced [i:ən]):

Harmonie [harmo'ni:]   **Harmonien** [harmo'ni:ən]
Symphonie [zYmfo'ni:]   **Symphonien** [zYmfo'ni:ən]
Melodie [melo'di:]   **Melodien** [melo'di:ən]

German also uses many French words and some English words. Such words are pronounced as in the original language:

Regie [reʒi]   **Regisseur** [reʒisœ:r]   **Souffleur** [suflœ:r]   **Parfum** [parfœ̃]

● **Word Lists—Monosyllabic and Irregular Words**

The following lists are meant to be used for quick reference in helping to determine vowel quality in monosyllabic words and irregular polysyllabic words. Recurring suffixes are also included. The lists are not necessarily exhaustive, and new words should be added as they are encountered. Many of these words are extremely common and should be memorized.

Words with [i:]

mir
dir
wir
ihn

Words with [I]

bin, bist   ich
mit   mich
hin   dich
in, im

ihm

-*in* (**Königin,** etc.)
-*ig* (**selig,** etc.)
-*nis* (**Bildnis,** etc.)
-*lich* (**endlich,** etc.)
-*isch* (**kindisch,** etc.)
-*ling* (**Jüngling,** etc.)

Words with [u:]

nur	zur (zu der)
nun	tun (tust, tut)
gut	Mut
Hut	Flut
Fluch	Tuch
Buch	suchen
husten	Gruß
Buß	Fuß
genug	klug
Geburt	-*mut* (**Anmut,** etc.)

-*tum* (**Heiligtum,** etc.)

Words with [U]

um
zum (zu dem)
durch
Kuß
Schluß
Fluß
Sucht (Sehnsucht, etc.)
Luther ['lUtɐ]
-*ung* (**Regung,** etc.)
un- (**Unschuld,** etc.)

Words with [o:]

vor	empor
Trost (also trösten [ø])	
Los (also -*los*)	
hoch (höchst [ø])	
groß	bloß
Schoß	Stoß (stoßen, stößt [ø])
Ostern	Kloster
Mond	Ton
Tod	tot
Not	Strom
Rom	Dom
Obst	Lob
Vogt	Hof (höflich [ø])
Schloße (meaning *hail*)	

Words with [ɔ]

von
vom (von dem)
ob
doch
noch
Hochzeit
Schloß (Schlösser [œ])
worden
geworden

Words with [y:]

süß
grüßen
büßen
Wüste
düster

Words with [Y]

küssen
müssen

Words with [e:]

dem	den
wem	wen
stets	Krebs
regnen	segnen
begegnen	Weg (noun)
Dresden ['dre:zdən]	
Petrus	

Words with [ɛ]

es
des
wes
weg (adverb)
Hexe
empor

Words with [e:r]

er	der
wer	wert
erst	Erde
Erz	Herd
Schwert	schwer
Pferd	werden
her (stressed)	

Words with [ɛr]

gern
Werk
ernst
erben
Herz
Schmerz
Lerche
fertig
her (unstressed)
Erz- (**Erzbischof**)
er-, ver-, zer-

Words with [a:]

nach	Schmach	Gemach	
Sprache		sprach (sprechen)	
brach (brechen)		stach (stechen)	
Maß	Straße	Spaß	aß (essen)
Tag	Tat	Jagd	Magd
Art	Bart	zart	Artzt
war	habt	kam (kommen)	
Mal	Tal	Qual	Schaf
Adler	Papst	Schlaf	Bratsche
Grab	Gras	Wagner	

Leichnam ['laeçna:m]   Heirat ['haera:t]
Heimat ['haema:t]   *-sal* (**Labsal,** etc.)
-sam (**langsam,** etc.)   *-bar* (**wunderbar,** etc.)

Words with [a]

Bach	Dach
Nacht	schwach
ach	rasch
naß	Gasse
an	am
ab	man
hat	hast
das	daß
Monat ['mo:nat]	

Diphthongs and Adjacent Vowels

German has three diphthongs. Two IPA renderings are commonly found for each:

- [ae] or [ai], which may be spelled *-ai-* as in **Hain** and **Mai,** *-ei-* as in **mein** and **Geist,** *-ay-* as in **Bayreuth,** *-ey-* as in **Meyer**
- [ao] or [au], which is spelled only *-au-* as in **auf** and **Haus**
- [ɔø] or [ɔy], which may be spelled *-eu-* as in **euch** and **Freude,** *-äu-* as in **Säule** and **Fräulein**

The first is used by Siebs (though using [ae] and [ao]), the second by Duden and others. The difference in the IPA rendering is in the second, glide-off sound of the diphthong, which reflects the difficulty in precisely defining this very short sound. The English equivalents of these sounds are rendered [aI], [aU], and [ɔI], suggesting a less tense, less pure glide-off sound after the main vowel than in German. Compare **mein** and **mine**, **Haus** and **house**, **keusch** and **coin**. The second vowel of German diphthongs is always late and short. There is never the possibility of separating the two sounds over two notes, as can happen in Italian.

This text will use the Siebs IPA alternative for German diphthongs. Although it might seem logical to insert a colon between the IPA symbols for German diphthongs (to indicate the much greater length of the first sound) it is not traditionally done.

Sometimes in German spelling two successive vowel-letters do *not* result in a diphthong. The most common example is *-ie-*, already discussed. Occasionally alternative spellings of the umlaut vowels are seen: *-ae-* for *ä*, *-oe-* for *ö*, *-ue-* for *ü*. An example of this is the name **Goethe** [gø:tə].

Vowel-letters can be adjacent but in different syllables, thus taking their individual sounds. In German words this can happen with a prefix followed by a stem beginning with a vowel:

beobachten [bəˈoːbaxtən] **beenden** [bəˈɛndən] **geändert** [gəˈɛndɐt]

and in German words derived from Latin and Greek:

Theater [teˈaːtɐ] **intellektuell** [Intɛlɛktuˈɛl]

including words ending *-ion* and *-ient*, in which the *i* acts as a glide:

Nation [naˈtsjoːn] **Aktion** [akˈtsjoːn] **Patient** [paˈtsjɛnt]

The Glide [j]

The only glide, or semiconsonant, in German is [j]. It is spelled with the letter *j*. At first glance, this German sound seems to be equivalent to English [j] spelled with *y* as in **yes**. Although the IPA symbol is the same, there is an important difference between the sounds. The English version is a rapid [i]. The German version is described by Siebs as a voiced [ç]. It therefore has a more concentrated airflow than English *y*. (It must not, however, sound like English *j* as in **jump**.)

ja [ja]	**jetzt** [jɛtst]	**Jammer** ['jamɐ]
Jüngling ['jʏŋlIŋ]	**Majestät** [majɛs'tɛːt]	

In words of foreign origin that spell this glide with *i*, as in **Familie** [fa'miːljə] and **Nation** [na'tsjoːn], Siebs (and others) uses a different IPA symbol, either [i] or [ĭ]. This is logical, since the sound is not the same as the one described above. However, most texts and dictionaries use [j] in these words; this text does also.

In words of French origin, *j* is pronounced [ʒ]:
Journal [ʒurnaːl], **Jalousie** [ʒaluzi].

Consonants

● **Double Consonants**

In spoken German, double consonants are not particularly lengthened as they are in Italian. In *sung* German, however, they often are. This is especially true in slower, more sustained singing, where the lengthened consonant sound helps to imply the short vowel sound preceding it.

IPA transcription for German does not normally use two consonant symbols to indicate a lengthened sound for German. Nevertheless, the student should listen carefully to German and Austrian singers to develop a sense of when a subtle lengthening of the double consonant is appropriate.

The following lists compare similarly spelled words with single and double consonants. In speaking these words, the essential difference will be in the vowel quality and length in the stressed syllable.

ihre ['iːrə]	**irre** ['Irə]
hehren ['heːrən]	**Herren** ['hɛrən]
fühlen ['fyːlən]	**füllen** ['fʏlən]
bieten ['biːtən]	**bitten** ['bItən]
Sohne ['zoːnə]	**Sonne** ['zɔnə]
Höhle ['høːlə]	**Hölle** ['hœlə]

Note: When the combination *-ck-* is divided syllabically, as it often is in musical scores, it is spelled *k-k*: **blicken** becomes **blik-ken**, **Locken** becomes **Lok-ken**.

Sometimes students make the mistake of spelling such words with double *kk*, a combination that otherwise exists only rarely in German (as in **Akkord**).

● Phrasal Doublings

In German (as in English) this term refers to the lengthening of a consonant sound when it ends one word and begins the next word within a phrase:

dein Name   dem Meere   der Tag kommt

The same phenomenon occurs between elements of compound words:

Nebelland   niederrinnen   Festtag   Bettdecke

In such cases the consonant sound should be prolonged in the manner of Italian double consonants. The amount of prolongation depends on context, primarily the amount of time allowed by the musical setting.

● CH

This combination has two pronunciations in German: [x] and [ç].

- [x]: Germans call this the "ach-Laut" (**Laut** means "sound"). The tongue is in the position for the vowel [a]. An unvoiced airstream is focused at the back of the hard palate. It occurs when -*ch*- follows "back" vowels: *a, o, u,* and *au*.

  Bach [bax]   **doch** [dɔx]   **Buch** [buːx]   **auch** [aox]

- [ç]: Germans call this the "ich-Laut." The tongue is in the position for [I] or [i]. An unvoiced airstream focuses just behind the upper teeth. It occurs when -*ch*- follows all vowels and diphthongs except the above: *i, e, ä, ö, ü, ie, ei, eu, äu*.

mich [mIç]	**Becher** [ˈbɛçɐ]	**rächen** [ˈrɛçən]
Köcher [ˈkœçɐ]	**Bücher** [ˈbyːçɐ]	**Reich** [raeç]
euch [ɔøç]	**räuchern** [ˈrɔøçɐn]	

  Important: This sound is also used when -*ch*- follows consonants:

  Milch [mIlç]   **manche** [mançə]   **durch** [durç]

including the common diminutive suffix -*chen*:

Liebchen ['li:pçən] **Mädchen** ['mɛ:tçən] **Häuschen** ['hɔøsçən]

To ears that are unused to this sound, [ç] can sound like [ʃ], but they are different and distinct sounds.

Both [x] and [ç] are light and of short duration. Nonnatives often overemphasize them, especially [x].

In words of Greek origin -*ch*- is usually pronounced [k]:

Chor [ko:ɐ] **Orchester** [ɔɐ'kɛstɐ] **Charakter** [ka'raktɐ]

although it is sometimes [ç]:

China ['çi:na]   **Cherub** ['çe:rUp] **Chemie** [çe'mi:]
Psychologie [psyçolo'gi:] **Echo** ['ɛço]

When it begins German proper names it is [k]:

Chiemsee ['ki:mze:] **Chemnitz** ['kɛmnits] (however
Chamisso, originally a French name, is [ʃa'mIso])

● **CHS**

Occasionally in German the combination -*chs*- occurs as one element within the stem. In this case it is pronounced [ks]:

Fuchs [fUks]   **Sachs** [zaks]   **Ochs** [ɔks]
Lachs [laks]   **wachsen** ['vaksən] **wechseln** ['vɛksəln]

The word **sechs** is [zɛks] but **sechzehn** is ['zɛçtse:n] and **sechzig** is ['zɛçtsIç]. The combination *chs* as [ks] happens in relatively few words, however.

Most of the time when the spelling -*chs*- occurs, the *ch* ends the word stem and the *s* is part of a word ending. In such cases the *ch* and the *s* are to be pronounced separately. This is often difficult for nonnatives. There are four situations in which *ch* and *s* must be pronounced as separate elements:

1. -*ch* plus verb ending -*st*: **du lachst** [laxst],
   du brichst [brIçst], **du suchst** [zu:xst]
2. -*ch* plus genitive *s*: **des Bachs** [baxs], **des Reichs** [raeçs]
3. -*ch* plus superlative suffix -*st*: **höchst** [hø:çst],
   herrlichster ['hɛrlIçstɐ]
4. Compound words: **nachsuchen** ['na:xzu:xən]

One word seems to cause particular difficulty for many people. This word is **nichts** [nɪçts]. In some dialects (and in the libretto of *Der Rosenkavalier*) this word is spelled and pronounced "nix." Except for these special circumstances, the word must be pronounced properly. Some practice may be required to do so.

Die Entführung aus dem Serail (Mozart)

Nichts, nichts, nichts, nichts— soll mich er - schüttern
[nɪçts]   [zɔl mɪç ɛɐ'ʃʏtɐn]

Matthäus-Passion (Bach)

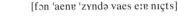

von ei - ner— Sün- de weiß er nichts, nichts
[fɔn 'aenɐ 'zʏndə vaes eːɐ nɪçts]

● **R**

There are two essential ways of dealing with the letter *r* for the purposes of singing German:

1. Excluding prefixes, *r* should be pronounced with a flip of the tongue whenever it precedes a vowel. The usual IPA symbol for this is [r] (used by Siebs and Duden), although [ɾ] (as for Italian) may be encountered:

Türen ['tyːrən] **Trost** [troːst] **lehren** ['leːrən] **Regen** ['reːgən]

Rolling the *r* is appropriate when emphasis is needed, although not for intervocalic *r* (unless it is doubled, as in **irren**).

2. In all other situations, that is, when *r* precedes a consonant, ends a word, or ends a prefix, the *r* may be flipped *or* it may become a vowel sound similar to, but distinct from, schwa. There are two accepted IPA symbols for this sound: [ɒ] and [ɐ]. This text uses [ɐ], as used by Siebs and Duden. The sound of this [ɐ] is darker than [ə] and it is always short, often extremely short.

    der [deːɐ] or [deːr]   **mir** [miːɐ] or [miːr]
    nur [nuːɐ] or [nuːr]
    vergessen [fɛɐ'gɛsən] or [fɛr'gɛsən]   **ernst** [ɛɐnst] or [ɛrnst]

In the above examples, the vowel before the *r* receives its usual sound, then the *r* is either flipped or pronounced [ɐ].

When -er (or -er plus consonant) ends a *polysyllabic* word or word stem, the IPA rendering is either [ər] or [ɐ]. In the second version, the r is incorporated into the vowel sound. [ɐ] can never follow schwa.

Lieder ['liːdɐ] or ['liːdər]   **zittern** ['tsItɐn] or ['tsItərn]
unser ['Unzɐ] or ['Unzər]   **linderst** ['lIndɐst] or ['lIndərst]
Biedermeier ['biːdɐmaeɐ] or ['biːdərmaeər]

Treating r as a vowel sound in this way happens in English, particularly British English, so the concept is not unfamiliar. German singers are not consistent among themselves as to how to treat r, and often either solution could be appropriate. The choice will be influenced by context, musical and literary style, and individual taste.

The pronunciation of r with the uvula (IPA symbol [R]) is used extensively in German speech, but, as with French, it is not considered appropriate for singing.

● B, D, G

These three consonants normally take the voiced sounds [b], [d], [g], familiar from English and other languages:

lieben ['liːbən]   **leiden** ['laedən]   **liegen** ['liːgən]

When final in a word, part of a final consonant cluster, or final in a word stem followed by a consonant, these consonants lose their voiced quality and become devoiced [p], [t], [k]:

Liebchen ['liːpçən]   **Leid** [laet]   **liegt** [liːkt]
endlos ['ɛntloːs]   **klagst** [klaːkst]   **selbst** [zɛlpst]

When final in a stem followed by a vowel, voicing is retained:

Mond [moːnt] but **Monde** ['moːndə]   **Mondeslicht** ['moːndəslIçt]

Both Siebs and Duden use the IPA symbols [p], [t], [k] for the devoiced versions of *b*, *d*, and *g*, but other experts make a distinction between, for example, devoiced *b* and [p]. The devoiced sounds are generally gentler and less plosive than their unvoiced counterparts. To indicate this distinction, a different symbol can be used, namely [b̥], [d̥], [g̥].

This text will follow the example of Siebs and Duden for IPA, but it is important to devoice these sounds in an unexaggerated manner. This is particularly essential when the devoicing occurs medially: words such as **ewiglich** and **endlich** should connect the devoiced consonant to the following consonant smoothly, with no separation or aspiration.

When devoicing occurs at the end of words with long vowels, the singer must be sure that an exaggerated devoicing does not shorten the vowel: **Tag** must be pronounced [taːk] or [taːg̊] and not [tak].

A certain family of words whose basic forms end in -el, -en, and -er seems to constitute an exception to the above rule. When such words take endings, the e is dropped. If the preceding consonant is b, d, or g, they retain their voiced quality, as if the e were still there. Another way to view it is that the l, n, or r ends the stem, not the preceding b, d, or g.

übel [ˈyːbəl]	**edel** [ˈeːdəl]	**eigen** [ˈaegən]	**ander** [ˈandər]
übler [ˈyːblɐ]	**edler** [ˈeːdlɐ]	**eigner** [ˈaegnɐ]	**andrer** [ˈandər]
üble [ˈyːblə]	**edle** [ˈeːdlə]	**eigne** [ˈaegnə]	**andre** [ˈandrə]
übles [ˈyːbləs]	**edles** [ˈeːdləs]	**eignes** [ˈaegnəs]	**andres** [ˈandrəs]

The noun **Gold** is [gɔlt] but the adjective **golden** [ˈgɔldən] retains a voiced d in all forms (**goldner, goldne, goldnes**). Similarly, **Wagner** (from **Wagen**) is pronounced [ˈvaːgnɐ] not [ˈvaːknɐ].

Unrelated to the above, and a special case, is the verb **widmen** [ˈvɪtmən] and the noun **Widmung** [ˈvɪtmʊŋ]. The devoicing of the d is irregular. The word **kindisch** is [ˈkɪndɪʃ]. The d irregularly does not devoice.

● **The Suffix -IG**

In this common suffix, g functions differently. When final, or followed by a consonant in the same word, this suffix is pronounced [ɪç]:

heilig [ˈhaelɪç]	**heiligt** [ˈhaelɪçt]	**selig** [ˈzeːlɪç]
seligste [ˈzeːlɪçstə]	**König** [ˈkøːnɪç]	**Königs** [ˈkøːnɪçs]
ewig [ˈeːvɪç]	**Ewigkeit** [ˈeːvɪçkaet]	

When this suffix is followed by a vowel in the same word, the g returns to its normal voiced sound:

heiligen [ˈhaelɪgən] **seliger** [ˈzeːlɪgɐ] **Königin** [ˈkønɪgɪn] **ewige** [ˈeːvɪgə]

When this suffix is followed in turn by the suffixes -lich or -reich, the g devoices to [k]. The reason is one of euphony, so that [ç] does not occur twice in the same word:

ewiglich [ˈeːvɪklɪç] **Königreich** [ˈkœnɪkraeç] **wonniglich** [ˈvɔnɪklɪç]

One hears deviations from the above in colloquial German as spoken in different parts of German-speaking countries. These are the rules for **Bühnendeutsch**, however, and should be observed by singers.

● S

Excluding the combinations listed in the next section, s has two sounds: voiced [z], unvoiced [s].
  s is voiced [z] in the following situations:

- Beginning a word when followed immediately by a vowel: **singen** ['zɪŋən], **sauber** ['zaobɐ], **sein** [zaen]

(*Note*: Some German speakers use [s] for these words; however [z] is recommended.)

- Intervocalic: **böse** ['bø:zə], **Esel** ['e:zəl], **Hause** '[haozə]
- After a voiced consonant and preceding a vowel: **unser** ['Unzɐ], **Amsel** ['amzəl], **also** [al'zo]
- The suffixes **-sam** and **-sal** regardless of what precedes them (many German speakers do not observe this): **einsam** ['aenza:m], **Schicksal** ['ʃɪkza:l], **Labsal** ['la:pza:l]

s is unvoiced [s] in the following situations:

- At the end of a word: **Haus** [haos], **ans** (an das) [ans], **uns** [Uns]
- After an unvoiced consonant: **Rätsel** ['rɛ:tsəl], **gipsen** ['gɪpsən]
- Before any consonant (excluding combinations in next section): **lispeln** ['lɪspəln], **fast** [fast]

Important: When s links parts of a compound word (genitive *s*) it is *always* unvoiced, even when following a voiced consonant. Such words are frequently mispronounced:

Lebensreise ['le:bənsraezə]	*not*	[	zraezə]
Himmelsblau ['hImməlsblao]	*not*	[	zblao]
Frühlingsblüten ['fry:lɪŋsbly:tən]	*not*	[	zbly:tən]

● SCH

When part of the same syllable, the combination *sch* always forms [ʃ]:

Schule ['ʃu:lə]	**rasch** [raʃ]	**Schein** [ʃaen]
löschen ['lœʃən]	**waschen** ['vaʃən]	**Tasche** ['taʃə]
Botschaft ['bo:tʃaft]		

When *s* and *ch* are adjacent, the *s* sometimes ends the stem and the *ch* begins a suffix. The result is [sç], a difficult combination for English speakers. This happens almost exclusively with the diminutive suffix *-chen*: **Häuschen** ['hɔøsçən], **Röschen** ['rø:sçən].

When *s* and *h* occur together in German they are always in different syllables (different word elements) and therefore to be pronounced separately. Do not confuse this situation with English *sh*: **boshaft** ['bo:shaft], **Gotteshaus** ['gɔtəshaos].

● **ST, SP**

When these combinations are at the beginning of a word or word stem they are pronounced [ʃt] and [ʃp]:

stellen ['ʃtɛlən]	**Stirn** [ʃtɪʁn]
zerstören ['tsɛɐʃtø:rən]	**Strudel** ['ʃtru:dəl]
Auferstehung ['aofɛɐʃte:Uŋ]	**spinnen** ['ʃpInən]
Sprache ['ʃpra:xə]	**Gespräch** [gə'ʃprɛ:ç]
entsprechen [ɛnt'ʃprɛçən]	

When these combinations are *not* at the beginning of a word or stem they are pronounced [st] and [sp]. It is a common mistake to assume that all such occurrences are pronounced with [ʃ]. Learn to recognize word elements to determine which pronunciation is correct:

beste ['bɛstə]	**schnellste** ['ʃnɛlstə]
gestern ['gɛstɐn]	**Postamt** ['pɔstamt]
Gastspiel ['gastʃpi:l]	**Wespe** ['vɛspə]
Knospe ['knɔspə]	**lispeln** ['lIspəln]
Liebestreu ['li:bəstrɔø]	**austragen** ['aostra:gən]
auspacken ['aospakən]	

● **H, V, W, X**

At the beginning of a word or stem, *h* is given its customary sound (familiar from English) produced by a short voiceless air flow:

Hauch [haox] **holen** ['ho:lən] **Gehalt** [gə'halt] **erheben** [ɛɐ'he:bən]

The same sound occurs in the suffixes *-heit* and *-haft*:

Schönheit ['ʃø:nhaet] **Hoheit** ['ho:haet] **lebhaft** ['le:phaft]

When *h* follows a vowel within a stem it is silent, but renders the preceding vowel closed and/or long:

sehen ['ze:ən]	**ruhig** ['ru:Iç]	**Höhe** ['hø:ə]
sehr [ze:ɐ]	**ihr** [i:ɐ]	**wahr** [va:r]

In words of Germanic origin, *v* is almost always found at the beginning of a word or stem and is pronounced [f]:

Vogel ['fo:gəl]   **Veilchen** ['faelçən]   **davon** [da'fɔn] **unvergeßlich** ['Unfɛɐgɛsllç]

One example of medial -*v*- is **Frevel** ['fre:fəl] and derivatives.
In most words of foreign origin, *v* is pronounced [v]:

Klavier [kla'vi:ɐ]   **privat** [pri'va:t]   **Universität** [univɛrzi'tɛ:t]

Although when final it devoices to [f]:

brav [bra:f]   **Motiv** [mo'ti:f]   **intensiv** [Intɛn'zi:f]

The letter *w* is always pronounced [v]:

Wein [vaen]   **zwei** [tsvae]   **schwarz** [ʃvarts]   **weh** [ve:]

except in proper names ending in -*ow* when it is silent:

Bülow ['by:lo]   **Lützow** ['lYtso]

The letter *x* is always pronounced [ks]. It has the effect of two consonants, thus causing the preceding vowel to be open:

Nixe ['nIksə]   **Exemplar** [ɛksɛm'pla:r]   **Hexe** ['hɛksə]

● **Z, TZ, SZ, C**

The letter *z* is always pronounced [ts]:

Zug [tsu:k]   **Zigeuner** [tsï'gɔønɐ]   **Lenz** [lɛnts]   **verzehren** [fɛr'tse:rən]

There is no difference in pronunciation between *z* and *tz*. Both are [ts]. This is true even when *t* and *z* are in different word elements, as in the last two examples below. Siebs and Duden differ slightly in how they transcribe such cases, but both imply that it is incorrect to give a separate articulation to the *t* and then pronounce [ts]:

setzen ['zɛtsən]   **jetzt** [jɛtst]   **entzwei** [ɛn'tsvae]   **entzücken** [ɛn'tsYkən]

The combination *sz* is rare. Each letter takes its own sound, [sts]:

Szene ['stse:nə]   **szenisch** ['stse:nIʃ]   **faszinieren** [fastsini:rən]

In words of Germanic origin, the letter *c* is found only in combination with other consonant-letters (*ck, sch*). In words of foreign origin, *c* can stand alone as a single consonant. Initial *c* before *i*, *e*, or *ä* is also [ts] (sometimes such words are spelled with z):

Citrone [tsI'tro:nə]   **Cäsar** ['tsɛ:zar]   **Ces** [tsɛs]   **Cäcilie** [tsɛ'tsi:ljə]

Before *a*, *o*, and *u* the pronunciation of *c* is [k]: **Café** [ka'fe].

● **Other Consonant Combinations**

There are many other consonant combinations in German. The following is a guide to their pronunciation.

- *gn* is pronounced [gn] (the *g* is not silent as in English): **Gnade** ['gna:də], **gnädige** ['gnɛ:digə].
- *kn* is pronounced [kn] (the *k* is not silent as in English): **Knie** [kni], **Knoten** ['kno:tən], **Knödel** ['knø:dəl], **knapp** [knap].
- *ng* is pronounced [ŋ] as in English *singer*. It is never [ŋg] as in English *finger*: **lang** [laŋ], **Finger** ['fIŋɐ], **Sänger** ['zɛŋɐ].
- *nk* is pronounced [ŋk] just as in English: **danken** ['daŋkən], **Frankreich** ['fraŋkraeç], **Bank** [baŋk].
- *pf* is pronounced [pf]. When initial, the [p] sound is very light and quick: **Pferd** [pfe:ɐt], **Pforte** ['pfɔrtə], **Pfingsten** ['pfIŋstən], **Kopf** [kɔpf].
- *ps* is pronounced [ps]. The *p* is never silent as in English: **Psalm** [psalm], **Psychologie** [psyçolo'gi:].
- *ph* is pronounced [f] as in English. It functions as one consonant in determining the length of the preceding vowel: **Philosoph** [filo'zo:f], **Phrase** ['fra:zə].
- *qu* is pronounced [kv]. It is never [kw] as in English: **Qual** [kva:l], **Quelle** ['kvɛlə], **Quartier** [kvar'ti:r].
- *th* is pronounced [t] when both letters are part of the same element: **Theater** [te'a:tɐ], **Apotheke** [apo'te:kə]. Sometimes old German uses *th* where modern German uses only *t*: **Theil—Teil** [tael], **Rath—Rat** [ra:t]. If *t* and *h* belong to different word elements, they are pronounced separately: **Rathaus** ['ra:thaos], **Gottheit** ['gɔthaet].
- *ti* is pronounced [tsj] in the suffixes *-tion* and *-tient*: **Nation** [na'tsjo:n], **Aktion** [ak'tsjo:n], **Patient** [pa'tsjɛnt].
- *tsch* is pronounced [tʃ] as in English **church**. This is the only way to spell this sound in German: **Deutsch** [dɔøtʃ], **tschechisch** ['tʃɛçIʃ], **Quatsch** [kvatʃ].

Glottal Attacks

A characteristic of German, as of English, is that words that begin with a vowel are usually initiated with a light glottal stroke. The

IPA symbol for this is [ǀ] (used by both Siebs and Duden) or [ʔ]. Compare in English:

announce [ǀəˈnaƱns]   an ounce [ǀænǀaƱns]

Say these German phrases using a gentle glottal attack on each word that begins with a vowel:

Er ist ein alter Mann	[ǀeɐ ǀɪst ǀaen ˈaltɐ man]
In einem Augenblick	[ǀɪn ˈaenəm ˈaogənblɪk]
Ich unglücksel'ger Atlas	[ǀɪç ˈƱnglƱkzeːlgɐ ˈatlas]

Moreover, such glottal separation is required in German when a word stem begins with a vowel; that is, when a prefix immediately precedes a vowel, and when elements within a compound word begin with a vowel:

geändert [gəˈɛndɐt]	**verantworten** [fɛɐˈantvɔrtən]
beobachten [bəˈoːbaxtən]	**Abendessen** [ǀˈabəntǀɛsən]
erinnern [ǀɛɐˈɪnɐn]	**eigenartig** [ǀˈaegənǀartɪç]

An exception to this is found in compound adverbs beginning with *her-*, *hin-*, *dar-*, *vor-*, and *wor-*, as well as the isolated word **warum**. In such words there is no glottal separation before the second element:

| **herein** [hɛˈraen] | **hinab** [hɪˈnap] | **daran** [daˈran] |
| **vorüber** [foˈryːbɐ] | **worauf** [voˈraof] | |

However, similar constructions formed from elements other than the above will take the glottal stroke:
bergab [bɛrkǀˈap], **bergan** [bɛrkǀˈan].

Though Siebs and Duden indicate otherwise, the prefix *un-* also commonly connects through a vowel: **unaufhörlich** [ˈUnaofhørlɪç], **unendlich** [Unˈɛntlɪç], though this is dependent on how the word is emphasized in context.

Glottal Separation versus Legato Connection in Singing German

In singing, glottal strokes should be light and quick so as not to detract from the legato line. It is often permissible, even desirable, to eliminate the glottal separation altogether. The singer should also develop the skill of releasing final consonants and articulating a following vowel with a subtle lift that implies a brief glottal separation but is different from a true glottal.

When to employ the glottal and when not to is a complex issue. The singer is constantly faced with a variety of such situations in German. Decisions will be influenced by musical style, tempo, and the relative importance of musical or textual considerations at that particular moment. In listening to native German-speaking singers, one commonly hears elimination of glottals to enhance legato. With *Lieder* this is probably the rule rather than the exception, but do not be surprised to hear different solutions to the same phrase, since there is no absolute uniformity on this point, just as there is no absolute uniformity on pronouncing *r* with a flip of the tongue or as [ɐ].

Until the singer develops a sense of when to use or omit glottal strokes, two rules of thumb are helpful to remember:

1. Important words in stressed positions, if they begin with a vowel, will likely take a glottal attack (there certainly are exceptions to this).
2. If by omitting a glottal stroke the meaning of a word is altered, or the clarity of the text is unduly compromised, the glottal stroke should be used.

It cannot be stressed enough that any glottal usage should be light.

Important words can be any part of speech, but here are some examples of nouns that would require a glottal separation:

Kriegers Ahnung (Schubert)

lag   sie   in   mei - nem **Arm**
[laːk zi ɪn 'maenəm ǀ arm]

Wie Melodien (Brahms)

und   führt   es   vor   das   **Aug**
[ʊnt fyːrt ɛs foːr das ǀ aok]

Vier ernste Gesänge (Brahms)

so   wär   ich   ein   tö - nend_   **Erz**
[zo veːr ɪç aen 'tøːnənt ǀ eːrts]

Verbal separable prefixes are usually important and stressed within a phrase. If the prefix begins with a vowel it probably will require a glottal separation:

Frauenliebe und Leben (Schumann)

Sü - ßer Freund, du blick est mich verwund-ert **an**
[ˈzyːsɐ frɔønt du ˈblɪkəst mɪç fɛɐˈvʊndɐt ǀ an]

Abschied (Schubert)

doch nim - mer wend ich mein Röß - lein **um**
[dɔx ˈnɪmɐ vɛnt ɪç maen ˈrœslaen ǀ ʊm]

Der neue Amadis (Wolf)

Als ich noch ein Kna - be war,
[als ɪç nɔx aen ˈknaːbə waːr]

sper - rte man mich **ein**
[ˈʃpɛrtə man mɪç ǀ aen]

In this last example, notice that **ein** occurs twice, once as an unstressed article and once as a stressed verbal prefix (**einsperren**). The first would not require a glottal separation, whereas the second would.

The examples given below present some other instances where the singer must decide whether a glottal separation is to be done. They are offered to raise awareness of the issue.

When *r* immediately precedes a word beginning with a vowel, a light flip into the subsequent vowel is often heard:

Intermezzo (Schumann)

und zu dir ei - lig zieht
[ʊnt tsu diːr̬ ˈaelɪç tsiːt] **or** [ʊnt tsu diːɐ ǀˈaelɪç tsiːt]

Die Stille (Schumann)

Ich wünscht, ich wär— ein Vög - lein
[ɪç vʏnʃt ɪç wɛːr‿aen 'føːk'laen] **or** [ɪç vʏnʃt ǀɪç wɛːɐ ǀaen 'føːk'laen]

Comparing these two examples, the first is more likely to employ a light glottal separation after the *r* because the next word (**eilig**) is stressed and emphasized in the musical setting. However, omission of the glottal and a flip of the *r* is still an option here. The second example shows the word following the *r* (**ein**) as short and unstressed and therefore unlikely to warrant a glottal stroke.

Was ist Sylvia? (Schubert)

ih - rem Aug'— eilt— A - mor zu—
['iːrəm ǀ aok aelt 'aːmoːɐ tsu]

Here are four successive words beginning with vowels, two of which occur after rests. At the beginning of a phrase, or after a rest within a phrase, glottal attacks should be used very judiciously, if at all. Concerning the other two words, it seems clear that **Aug'** should receive a light glottal separation, but with **Amor** this is less clear. The best solution is probably not a true glottal but a release of the *t* of **eilt**, which distinctly defines it as belonging to the preceding word rather than the following word. Certainly employing a glottal on all four words yields a very unmusical result.

weiß was— ich lei - de
[vaes vas‿ɪç 'laedə]

Nur wer die
Sehnsucht kennt
(Schubert)

In this example connection from **was** to **ich** is desirable since a glottal separation would emphasize **ich** too much, besides detracting from legato. As long as the s is not exaggerated, the intelligibility of **ich** is not compromised by connecting the words (though too much time on the *s* might convey **sich**).

Here are two examples in a faster tempo:

Vergebliches Ständchen (Brahms)

Gu-ten A - bend, mein Schatz, gu - ten A - bend mein Kind
['guːtən_'aːbənt maen ʃats 'guːtən_'aːbənt maen kɪnt]

Der Musensohn (Schubert)

So geht's von Ort zu Ort
[zo geːts vɔn l ɔrt_tsu_ɔrt]

In the first example, a clear glottal separation before **Abend** sounds unsatisfactory, probably because the note value is short. A connection of the preceding *n* is desirable, as long as it is light and unexaggerated. In the second example, by contrast, the glottal separation before the first occurrence of **Ort** is called for. Even a light connection of the preceding sound compromises the clarity of the text. The second occurrence, following a vowel, probably does not need a separation.

Phrasal Consonant Clusters

It was mentioned in the Italian section of this text that most Italian words end in vowels and many begin with vowels, resulting in the frequent occurrence of phrasal diphthongs and triphthongs. The opposite is true of German (and English). Most words begin with consonants and many end in consonants, resulting in frequent juxtaposition of consonant sounds. In many cases this simply requires the singer to clearly articulate adjoining sounds with no separation between them:

all mein   ich gehe   von dir   mit Kraft

If the first sound is a stop consonant (as with **mit** above) there may be a slight separation before the next sound, particularly if the note values are long enough.

Sometimes the phrasal clusters are more difficult because unfamiliar from English. This example from Schubert's *Winterreise* requires the clear articulation of [sts] for **es zieht:**

Gute Nacht (Schubert)

Es **zieht** ein Mon - den - schat - ten
[ɛs tsiːt aen ˈmoːndənʃatən]

Here the combination [nftb] is unusual; students often have trouble with the word **sanft**:

O wüsst ich doch (Brahms)

von Lie - be **sanft be** - deckt
[fɔn ˈliːbə zanft bəˈdɛkt]

A fairly common phrasal cluster is [çʃ]:

Das verlassene Mägdlein (Wolf)

ich schaue so da-rein
[ɪç ˈʃaoə zo daˈraen]

Ach Golgatha - Matthäus-Passion (Bach)

Die Un - schuld muß hier schul-**dig ster** - ben
[di ˈunʃult mʊs hiːr ˈʃʊldɪç ˈʃtɛrbən]

Am Feierabend (Schubert)

Was **ich schn**ei - de, was— **ich schl** - age
[vas ɪç ˈʃnaedə was ɪç ˈʃlaːgə]

Without separating the sounds, the singer must pronounce [ç] and move smoothly to [ʃ]. In the first two examples, the relatively leisurely tempo allows for easier execution than the third, at a considerably faster tempo. These examples (or similar ones) spoken slowly are an excellent means of getting students to clearly hear the difference between [ç] and [ʃ].

Still another case is [sʃ]:

Des Müllers Blumen (Schubert)

Wenn   al - **les schweigt**
[vɛn 'aləs ʃvaekt]

Der Frie - **dens- schluß**
[deːɐ 'friːdənsʃlus]

Am Abend da es kühle war-
Matthäus-Passion (Bach)

In the second example, the first *s* is a "genitive s" connecting two parts of a compound word. In all such occurrences, the [s] must be clear, even if very short, and must yield smoothly to [ʃ]. The lazy singer will omit [s] and pronounce [ʃ] only.

It must be said that sometimes consonant juxtapositions in German are particularly difficult to execute fully while maintaining musical quality within a particular musical setting. From the same Brahms song mentioned above:

O wüsst ich doch (Brahms)

Und **nichts zu** for - schen, **nichts**   **zu** späh'n
[unt nɪçts tsu 'fɔrʃən nɪçts tsu ʃpɛːn]

The words **nichts zu** contain the phrasal consonant cluster [çtsts]. One commonly hears [çts] only. With a light approach, it is possible to do the entire cluster.

Irrlicht (Schubert)

Al - les ein - es Irr - **lichts Spiel**
['aləs 'aenəs 'ɪrlɪçts ʃpiːl]

Similarly, this phrase contains [çtsʃp] (on a very short note value!). In performance the [s] tends to elide into the [ʃ].

The singer must learn to articulate consonant juxtapositions clearly, and the proper approach is to do them lightly. Such an approach will prevent the tongue from getting tied up in knots while maintaining musical line. Since German patterns are frequently different from English patterns, some practice may be required.

Possible Assimilation of Consonant Sounds

In situations involving the adjoining sounds [p] and [b], [k] and [g], [t] and [d], [s] and [z], another, more common possibility of consonant elision arises: **und der** is [Unt deːɐ], but should the [t] be fully released before articulating the [d]? In speech this would not happen, unless there were a pause between the words. In normal speech the tongue makes contact with the palate in one motion simultaneously for both sounds, initially devoiced for [t] but adding voiced quality as the tongue releases for [d]. The phrase **der Tag ging** would call for a similar simultaneous articulation of [k] and [g].

In singing, the tempo of the music and the style of the music will often determine whether such adjoining sounds should be articulated separately or simultaneously. The "heightened speech" nature of singing, which involves the need to project words clearly into a large space, results in far more separate articulations than does normal speech in such situations. Nevertheless, true legato singing often requires connection. The student should be aware of the possibilities and try out the alternatives to determine what yields the most satisfactory result in a given situation, initially in the presence of a teacher or a coach.

A common occurrence of phrasal [td] is in inversions of the **du** forms of verbs: **bist du**, **meinst du**, **lachst du**, etc. Certainly if the note values are short it is not necessary or desirable to separate the sounds:

Ach, ich fühls—Die Zauberflöte

fühlst du nicht   der Lie - be   Seh - nen
[fyːlst‿du nɪçt‿der (*or* [nɪçt der) ˈliːbə ˈzeːnən]

When the note values are longer, either solution is possible. Intelligibility is rarely an issue, so the singer must decide if separation otherwise enhances the phrase or not:

Kennst du das Land (Wolf)

Kennst— du   das Land
[kɛnst du das lant]

Die Götter Griechenlands (Schubert)

Schö - ne Welt,   wo   **bist— du?**
['ʃøːnə vɛlt vo bɪst du]

Heimliche Aufforderung (R. Strauss)

Doch **hast du** das Mahl—   ge - nos - sen
[dɔx hast du das maːl gə'nɔsən]

Und willst du deinen Liebsten sterben sehen (Wolf)

Und **willst du** dei - nen Lieb-sten ster - ben se - hen
[ʊnt vɪlst du 'daenən 'liːpstən 'ʃtɛrbən zeːən]

Here are some other examples to consider:

Nacht (R. Strauss)

Aus dem Wal - de **tritt die** Nacht
[aos deːm 'valdə trɪt di naxt]

In this case a separate articulation of the *t* before the *d* seems the best solution. Connection could compromise text intelligibility and does not particularly enhance legato line. The dotted rhythm also encourages placing the *t* distinctly on the second half of the second beat.

A bit later in the same song, however, connection seems the better choice:

Nacht (R. Strauss)

und **stiehlt die** Gar - ben weg vom Feld
[ʊnt ʃtiːlt‿di ˈɡarbən vɛk fɔm fɛlt]

The lack of a dotted rhythm gives less time, causing separation to sound fussy. The presence of the *l* before the *td* combination helps in allowing the word **stiehlt** to be understood clearly.

The tempo of this song makes separation undesirable, as well as virtually impossible:

Fort den ras - seln - den Trott!
[fɔrt‿deːn ˈrasəlndən trɔt]

An Schwager Kronos (Schubert)

Here are two examples of phrasal [kg]:

der‿ **Weg ge** - hüllt in Schnee
[deːr veːk‿ɡəˈhʏlt‿ɪn ʃneː]

Gute Nacht (Schubert)

Although the tempo here is moderate and separation is possible, nothing is gained by it. Connection certainly enhances legato, and textual clarity is not compromised.

Kindertotenlieder (Mahler)

Das Un-**glück ge** - schah‿ nur mir al - lein
[das ˈʊnɡlʏk ɡəˈʃaː nuːɐ miːr aˈlaen]

Here the slow tempo allows for the slight separation of the [k] and [g] sounds. The clarity of the text is also enhanced. The release of the [k] should not overwhelm the [g], however.

With phrasal [s] and [z], separation is rarely done because they are continuing sounds. Furthermore, it is very common to hear as-simimilation so that only a prolonged [s] is heard:

An die ferne Geliebte (Beethoven)

Was ge - schie- den **uns** **so** weit
[vas gə'ʃiːdən ʊns zo vaet]

When time allows and the affected words are important, the release should have voicing so that [z] is heard, however briefly:

An die Leier (Schubert)

Ich will von A - **treus'** **Söh**-nen
[ɪç vɪl fɔn 'aːtrɔøs 'zøːnən]

An eine Aeolsharfe (Wolf)

ge- heim - nis vol - **les** **Sai** - ten- spiel
[gə'haemnɪsfɔləs 'zaetənʃpiːl]

FRENCH

Introduction

Of the three languages presented in this book, French is by far the least phonetic. A phonetic language, such as Italian or German, is one whose pronunciation follows logically and consistently from its spelling. Italian and German are not entirely phonetic, of course, but they are much more so than either French or English. Unfortunately, the unphonetic nature of French is very different from that of English. This fact is one of the greatest hurdles that an English-speaking singer must overcome in mastering French pronunciation.

To achieve an intermediate level of proficiency with French diction, at least the following points must be mastered:

1. A thorough understanding of French spelling and the sounds resulting from those spellings
2. Purity (no diphthongs) of vowels
3. Appropriate "lift" or brightness to [a] and [ɛ]
4. The sounds of the four nasal vowels (including not sounding the *n* or *m*) and keeping the sounds distinct one from another
5. The proper formation of the mixed vowels
6. Forward articulation and nonaspiration of consonants
7. A basic understanding of liaison

It is up to the teacher to decide to what extent some of the fine points in this chapter should be applied to the class or individual in question. For those inexperienced with French it is doubtless too much. Also, many teachers and coaches prefer to dispense with the fine points represented by distinctions between, for example, bright and dark *a*, vocalic harmonization, and vowel length. Many teachers and coaches do make these distinctions, however. For the sake of thoroughness, this text presents these points.

International Phonetic Alphabet (IPA) Symbols for French

"Pure" Vowels

[a] **madame, femme**
[ɑ] **bas, âme**
[ɛ] **belle, clair**
[e] **j'ai, été, pied**
[ɔ] **homme, Fauré**
[o] **trop, beau, chaud**
[i] **vie, il dit, Guy**
[u] **toujours, amour**

"Mixed" Vowels

[y] **tu, du, rue**
[œ] **coeur, seul**
[ø] **deux, feu**
[ə] **le, se**cret, **par**lerai, di**sent**

Nasal Vowels

[ɑ̃] **vent, chan**ter, **blanc**
[ɛ̃] **vin, plein, bien, pain**
[õ] **vont, tom**ber
[œ̃] **hum**ble, par**fum**

Glides

[j] **ciel, travailler**
[w] **oui, croire**
[ɥ] **puis, ennui**

Plosive Consonants

[b] **beau**
[p] **peau**
[d] **de**
[t] **te**
[g] **goût**
[k] **coût**

Fricative Consonants

[v] **vain**
[f] **faim**
[s] **son, ce, leçon**
[z] **gazon, chose**
[ʃ] **chez, crèche**
[ʒ] **j'ai, neige**

Lateral Consonants

[l] [ll] **lequel, illusion**

Vibrant Consonants

[r] [rr] **rire, irréel**

Nasal Consonants

[m] [mm] **même, immédiat**
[n] [nn] **nonne, innocent**
[ɲ] **cygne, agneau**

Dictionaries

Fortunately, most French dictionaries of recent publication, whether French-English or French only, use the International Phonetic Alphabet for all entries. Any dictionary that does not use the IPA is to be avoided. Most of them do not indicate vowel length or word stress, but since these points can be consistently deduced, their absence is not important. (See discussion of vowel length and word stress on pp. 124, 125, 171, and 172.)

There are some discrepancies from one dictionary to another, virtually all of them involving differences regarding [e] and [ɛ] in certain situations. One of them concerns the combination *ai*, normally pronounced open [ɛ]. This combination can be considered closed [e] when the next syllable has a closed vowel:

baiser is transcribed [beze] or [bɛze]
baisser is [bese] or [bɛse]
maison is [mezõ] or [mɛzõ]
raison is [rezõ] or [rɛzõ]
plaisir is [plezi:r] or [plɛzi:r]
aisé is [eze] or [ɛze]
pays is [pei] or [pɛi]
paisible is [pezibl(ə)] or [pɛzibl(ə)]

Since this situation is similar to vocalic harmonization (q.v.), and vocalic harmonization is considered an option rather than a rule, it is best to consider the alternative pronunciations to the above words as equally valid options. For the purposes of singing, this text prefers the closed pronunciation, just as it prefers the observing of vocalic harmonization.

Other inconsistencies between dictionaries concern initial *ess*. Some dictionaries have [e] whereas others have [ɛ]. **Essaim** is [esɛ̃] or [ɛsɛ̃], **essor** is [eso:r] or [ɛsɔ:r]. This text uses the closed version.

There are also discrepancies with [a] and [ɑ]. The word **croire**, for example, is usually given with [ɑ], but some dictionaries give it with [a]. Also, for initial *irr-* some dictionaries give [rr], implying a lengthened sound, while others do not.

Sometimes one encounters pronunciations in one dictionary that are not found in others. For example, one dictionary gives initial *ex* plus a vowel or *h* as [egz]: **exemple** [egzã:pl(ə)], whereas the customarily accepted pronunciation of all words with initial *ex* is with [ɛ]: [ɛgzã:pl(ə)].

Diacritical Marks

A distinguishing characteristic of written French is the presence of four diacritical marks. They contribute greatly to the "look" of the language. It is important to have a clear understanding of these signs and in what ways they affect pronunciation.

Accent Grave (grave accent): è, à, où

The grave accent occuring over *e* renders it open [ɛ]: **lèvre** [lɛ:vr(ə)], **légère** [leʒɛ:r(ə)]. When it occurs over other vowels it has no effect on pronunciation.

Accent Aigu (acute accent): é

The acute accent occurs only over *e* and renders it closed [e]: **été** [ete], **passé** [pase]. Be aware that capital letters often omit diacriticals: **Nuits d'Etoiles** (étoiles).

Accent Circonflexe (circumflex): î, ê, â, ô, û, aî, oî, oû, aû

The circumflex affects pronunciation only with ê, â and ô.

> ê is always open [ɛ]: **rêve** [rɛ:v(ə)], **tête** [tɛ:t(ə)]
> ô is always closed [o]: **drôle** [dro:l(ə)], **le nôtre** [lə no:tr(ə)]
> â is usually dark [ɑ] with rare exceptions:
> **âme** [ɑ:m(ə)], **pâle** [pɑ:l(ə)]

Diérèse (dieresis) or *Tréma*: ï, ë, ÿ

The dieresis occurs over one of the above vowel-letters only when the vowel-letter follows another vowel-letter. It indicates hiatus, or separation of the vowel sounds. In the word **naïf** [naif], the dieresis requires the two vowel-letters to be pronounced separately, whereas in the word **maître** [mɛ:tr(ə)], the same two letters combine to make the sound [ɛ]. Other examples are **haïr** [ai:r], **foëne** [fɔɛn(ə)], **Boïeldieu** [bɔjɛldjø].

Rarely, the dieresis indicates that a vowel-letter is silent or has no phonetic function in the vowel group:

Saint-Saëns [sɛ̃sɑ̃:s]   **ciguë** [sigy]   **Staël** [stal]

Cédille (cedilla)

In addition to the above diacriticals, there is also the cedilla, which is the small mark found under a *c* when it is to be pronounced as [s] before *a*, *o*, or *u*.

ça [sa]   **garçon** [garsõ]   **reçu** [rəsy]

Definitions of Terms Relating to French Diction

● **Mute e**

In spoken French, when the letter *e* with no accent is the only vowel-letter in a syllable or ends a word, it is usually silent:

mouv(e)ment [muvmã]   **méd(e)cin** [medsɛ̃]   **vill(e)** [vil]   **un(e)** [yn]

It is also silent in the verb ending *-ent* (but not *-aient*), and in final *-es* (except in monosyllables):

aiment [ɛm]   **aimes** [ɛm]   **belles** [bɛl]

This silent vowel-letter is called mute *e*. In singing it is generally pronounced, transcribed as [ə] (schwa), and sounded as [œ] (see discussion of this sound on p. 135). Except for cases where schwa clearly must be pronounced (such as monosyllables **le, me**, etc.), this text will indicate mute *e* in parentheses: [(ə)].

● Elision

When a mute *e* ends a word and the next word begins with a vowel or *h*, the *e* is never sounded in speech or in singing. The consonant sound before the mute *e* connects directly to the vowel sound beginning the next word. This is different from liaison.

elle est [ɛlɛ] **comme a** [kɔma] **fatigue amoureuse** [fatig amurø:z(ə)]

In the cases of mute *e* spelled *-ent* or *-es*, speech will elide as above, but singing will usually pronounce the *e* (as schwa) and sound the otherwise silent *t* or *s* in liaison to the next word (see below).

● Liaison

Liaison is the sounding of a normally silent final consonant before a word beginning with a vowel or a so-called unaspirated *h* (see below). This is very common in French, and more common in singing than in speech. It does not happen in every instance where it might seem to be called for. (See p. 156 for a complete explanation.)

vous avez [vuzave] **mon amour** [mõnamu:r] **deux heures** [døzœ:r]

● Aspirated h, Unaspirated h

The letter *h* is always silent in French. When *h* begins a word it sometimes prevents liaison from the previous word. When an initial *h* prevents liaison it is called an aspirated *h* (*h* aspiré). When initial *h* allows liaison it is called unaspirated *h* (*h* inaspiré). There is no way to determine which one applies. Each word must be checked in a dictionary. (*Note*: Do not make the mistake of thinking that aspirated *h* makes an aspirated sound as in English or German. It does not.) The aspirated *h* may result in a light glottal attack.

- Unaspirated *h*: **les hommes** [lɛzɔm], **en hiver** [ãnivɛ:r]
- Aspirated *h*: **les haricots** [lɛ|ariko], **des haies** [dɛ|ɛ]

● Vocalic Harmonization

Vocalic harmonization is the rhyming of vowel sounds in adjoining syllables. The adjoining syllables can be in the same word or in different words. In French this happens only with two pairs of vowels: [ɛ] and [e]; [œ] (or [ə]) and [ø].

The context for vocalic harmonization is very specific. When one of the above open vowels is followed by its closed counterpart, the open vowel will close to rhyme with it. The opposite situation (closed followed by open) does *not* result in vocalic harmonization.

With [ɛ] and [e] the usual patterns are two:

1. When *-ai-* is followed by *-er-*, *-ez-*, or *-é-*:

   baiser [bɛze] becomes [beze]
   aimez [ɛme] becomes [eme]
   laissé [lɛse] becomes [lese]

2. When monosyllables such as **les**, **mes**, **tes**, **ces** are followed by a word with [e] in the first syllable:

   les étoiles [lɛzetwaːl(ə)] becomes [lezetwaːl(ə)]
   ces études [sɛzetyd(ə)] becomes [sezetyd(ə)]
   tes baisers [tɛ bɛze] becomes [tebeze]

(Note that in the last example vocalic harmonization can extend over three syllables.)

With [œ] or [ə] and [ø] vocalic harmonization falls within one word:

heureux [œrø] becomes [ørø]   **cheveux** [ʃəvø] becomes [ʃøvø]

Patterns over two words such as **je veux** [ʒə vø] and **tu ne peux** [ty nə pø] do not take vocalic harmonization.

Vocalic harmonization occurs in French speech but is not as-
sumed. French dictionaries' pronunciation transcription (whether IPA or some other system) will not reflect vocalic harmonization. It is com-
mon practice in singing; nevertheless it should not be considered a requirement but a recommendation to facilitate optimum vocalism. It need not be applied if it gets in the way of optimum vocalism.

Syllabification

Syllabification is presented early in the discussion of French be-
cause it is constantly referred to as the chapter progresses. Since it is rather involved, the teacher may wish to cover the specific sounds first and then return to syllabification. In any case, syllabification should be studied regularly until mastered.

Understanding syllabification is crucial in determining the pronunciation of French words. Two adjacent letters may be pronounced one way if they are in the same syllable and another way if they are in different syllables. French shares with Italian the important trait of being characterized by *open syllabification*, that is, syllables that end in vowels.

A complicating element in French syllabification is the mute *e*. In speech it usually is nonsyllabic; in singing it usually is syllabic. Since this is a textbook for singers, the following discussion will consider mute *e* syllabic but put it in parentheses in IPA.

● Vowel-Consonant-Vowel

In this common pattern, the syllable will divide before the consonant:

a-mour mai-son du-rer pa-ro-le mé-de-cin

● Adjacent Vowels

When adjacent vowel-letters form a single vowel sound, as frequently happens in French, they all belong to the same syllable:

deux [dø] **beau-té** [bo - te] **coeur** [kœːr] **tou-jours** [tu - ʒuːr]

Sometimes a vowel-letter will represent a glide. French has three glides, [j], [w], and [ɥ]. When a glide is intervocalic the syllable divides before the glide, otherwise the glide is part of the syllable of the vowel following it:

a-ïeux [a - jø] **vieux** [vjø] **nuit** [nɥi]
pui-ssant [pɥi - sɑ̃] **oi-seau** [wa - zo]

When *y* occurs between vowels it has a dual function, essentially that of a double *ii* with the syllables dividing between the *ii*'s. The function of the first *i* varies according to the vowel preceding it, but the second *i* always becomes the [j] glide:

voyage (voi-ia-ge) [vwajaːʒ(ə)] **payer** (pai-ier) [peje] **fuyez** (fui-ier) [fɥije]

In the word **pays** and words derived from it, *y* functions similarly, except the second *i* has a vowel function (note closed [e]):

pays (pai-is) [pei] **paysage** (pai-i-sa-ge) [peizaːʒ(ə)]

A frequent spelling of the [j] glide in French is -*ill* following another vowel. This can be particularly confusing for newcomers to French:

travailler (tra-va-iller) [travaje]   **cueillir** (cue-illir) [kœji:r]
mouillé (mou-ille) [muje]

When -*ill* does not follow a vowel it is [ij]:

fille (fi-lle) [fi:j(ə)]   **billet** (bi-llet) [bijɛ]

except in three words in which it is pronounced [il]:

mille [mil(ə)]   **ville** [vil(ə)]   **tranquille** [trãkil(ə)]

and derivatives

million [miljõ]   **village** [vila:ʒ(ə)]   **tranquillité** [trãkilite]

These three words can be remembered in the phrase **mille villes tranquilles** (a thousand tranquil towns).
When *ill* is initial in a word it is [ill] (no glide): **illuminer** [illymine]. When -*il* ends a word after a vowel it creates a diphthong. Usually the glide-off of the diphthong is transcribed with [j], sometimes with [ĭ]:

soleil (so-leil) [sɔlɛ:j]   **cercueil** (cer-cueil) [sɛrkœ:j]
travail (tra-vail) [trava:j]

There are a number of situations involving adjacent vowels in which it is not always clear whether a vowel or a glide is involved. Musical settings usually prefer the vowel and therefore the extra syllable. (See p. 167 for musical examples.)

- When the infinitive verb endings -*er* and -*ir* follow *i*, *u*, or *ou* in some words: **lier** [lje], **tuer** [tɥe], **é-pa-nouir** [epanwi:r]. (Dictionaries give these words with glides; musical settings usually set them with vowels.) Words of this pattern after a consonant plus *l* or *r* have no glide: **trou-er** [true], **pri-er** [prie], **ou-bli-er** [ublie]. (Some dictionaries give [ije] for these last two words.)
- When the noun/adjective ending -*et* follows a vowel: **rouet** [rwɛ], **muet** [mɥɛ]. (Dictionaries give these words with glides; musical settings usually set them as vowels.)
- In patterns *ua*, *ue*, *ui*, after a consonant plus *l* or *r*, the *u* is a vowel. Syllables divide after the *u*: **tru-and, cru-au-té, cru-el, flu-ide.**

- But in patterns *gu* plus vowel and *qu* plus vowel, the *u* is silent: **gue-rre, Guy, quel, quand, qui-tter** (A few exceptions: **aiguille** [ɛgɥiːj(ə)], **quatuor** [kwatɥɔːr]).
- Patterns *gueil* and *cueil* have [œj]:
  orgueil (or-gueil) [ɔrgœːj], **recueil** (re-cueil) [rəkœːj].

Adjacent vowel-letters forming different vowel sounds are in different syllables. Other than the situations described above, this can happen in two ways:

- Dieresis: **Tha-ïs, No-ël.**
- One of the adjacent vowels is *é* or *è*: **po-è-te, ré-u-ssi.**

● **Adjacent Consonants**

French can have two or three adjacent consonant-letters. Sometimes one or two of these are silent and are therefore not a factor in syllabification. When an *n* or an *m* indicates a nasal vowel, for example, it obviously remains in the syllable of the nasal vowel but is not sounded:

en-fant loin-tain hum-ble sin-cè-re

Similarly, *h* is always either silent or part of the combinations *ch* and *ph*. Except when initial, it cannot begin a syllable:

bo-nheur i-nhu-main go-thi-que

Sometimes consonant clusters will be in one syllable and sometimes they will separate syllabically. The general rule of thumb is whether *the cluster could begin a word*. If the answer is yes, the cluster remains together in the same syllable. This is true of combinations that represent one sound, such as *ch, ph,* and *sc* (before *i* or *e*), as well as of blended sounds that can begin a word:

pé-cheur pro-phè-te de-scen-dre pa-tri(e) vien-dra

If two adjacent consonants could not begin a word they divide into separate syllables:

par-tir ob-jet al-tier

Three adjacent consonants will follow the same rule of thumb by dividing according to whatever combination could begin a word, usually one plus two: **cher-cher, ar-bre.**

Double consonants present some special situations. Normally they do not divide, nor are they lengthened as in Italian:

do-nner [dɔne]   **pa-sser** [pɑse]   **a-ller** [ale]

(Printed French will divide between double consonants.) Although not usually indicated in dictionaries, in singing it is traditional to lengthen double consonants in initial *ill*, *imm*, *inn*, and *irr*. The syllables would then divide between the double consonants:

il-lu-sion [illyzjõ]   **im-men-se** [immɑ̃:s(ə)]   **in-no-cent** [innɔsɑ̃]
ir-re-gu-lier [irregylje]

Initial *emm* and *enn* also divide between the double consonants, but because the first (irregularly) indicates a nasal vowel and the second functions as a consonant. There is no lengthening:
em-me-ner [ɑ̃məne], **en-nui** [ɑ̃nɥi].
The word **ennemi** is an exception to the above: **e-nne-mi** [ɛnəmi].
    There is also syllabic division in *cc* and *gg* after *e* or *i* because two different consonant sounds result:
sug-gé-rer [sygʒere], **ac-cident** [aksidɑ̃].
    A special case is also presented by the letter *x*. Since it normally represents two consonant sounds (either [ks] or [gz]), the two sounds divide between the syllables:
exister (ex-i-ster) [ɛg-zi-ste], **extrème** (ex-trè-me) [ɛk-strɛ-m(ə)].
    When *x* is sounded in numerical words it is [s] or [z] and therefore functions syllabically as a single consonant:
sixième [sizjɛm(ə)], **soixante** [swasɑ̃:t(ə)].

Word Stress

In French words of two or more syllables, the final syllable always takes a light stress, not including final mute *e*. All other syllables are equally unstressed. It must be emphasized that the stress on the final syllable is light. Italian, German, and English all have much more emphatic stress patterns, and the lack of such emphasis in French is a special characteristic of the language. This characteristic has influenced composers setting French texts to music, particularly since Debussy.
    When individual words combine to form phrases and breath groups, the light stress falls on the final syllable of the final word (excluding mute *e*), the words preceding the final word thus losing their stress, although secondary stresses may occur. Just as in any language, a change of inflection, and therefore stress, may occur ac-

cording to the meaning the speaker wishes to convey. The general pattern of normal conversational French, however, is as described above.

Because of the regularity of stress in French words, French dictionaries do not indicate stress. This text follows that precedent.

Vowel Length

While books on French phonetics discuss vowel length, it has not been customary for singer's diction texts to do so. Although vowel length is not as crucial to the flavor of the French language as it is to Italian and German, in some contexts it certainly plays a role. Because it is not as crucial, it is discussed at the end of the chapter (p. 171). The IPA transcriptions throughout this text indicate long vowels with the customary colon [:].

Vowel Sounds and How They Are Spelled

French has fifteen vowel sounds and, counting schwa, sixteen IPA symbols that represent them. One of the greatest problems in learning French pronunciation is learning all of the possible spellings of the vowel sounds. The following pages will examine each vowel sound and present the possible spellings.

● [a]

This sound is equivalent to [a] in Italian and other Romance languages. The bright [a] occurs much more frequently than the dark [ɑ]. Since native speakers of English tend to pronounce this sound too darkly, it is necessary for them to make sure that it has enough brightness and "lift."

The sound [a] is spelled as follows:

- *a*: When not nasalized and the only vowel-letter in the syllable: **apparat** [apara] (except situations calling for dark [ɑ]; see next section)
- *à*: When the only vowel letter in the syllable: **là** [la]
- *oi*: Results in [wa] (except when nasalized): **oiseau** [wazo], **moi** [mwa], **fois** [fwa] (spelled *eoi* in the word **s'asseoir** [saswa:r])

- *oy*: results in [waj] (except when nasalized):
  royal [rwajal], **foyer** [fwaje], **voyons** [vwajõ]
- *e*: In medial *-emm* and *-enn*: **femme** [fam(ə)], **solennel**
  [sɔlanɛl], including adverbs in *-emment*:
  fréquemment [frekamã] **ardemment** [ardamã]; with exceptions: **flemme** [flɛm(ə)], **gemme** [ʒɛm(ə)]

In addition, there are some irregular spellings of [a]:

- *ao*: **paonne** [pan], **paonner** [pane]
- *oe*: **moelle** [mwal(ə)] (normally *oe* is part of *oeill* or *oeu* and
  sounds as [œ])

● [ɑ]

The dark [ɑ] sound is pronounced with a lower, more "back" ori-
entation than bright [a]. It occurs much less often than bright
[a]. Some pedagogues prefer to dispense with this sound altogether for singing. In any case, beginners with French should per-
fect the bright [a] before concerning themselves much with the
dark [ɑ].

There are four common situations resulting in dark [ɑ]:

1. *â* in all common words: **âme** [ɑ:m(ə)], **château** [ʃɑto],
   grâce [grɑ:s(ə)] (some subjunctive verb forms use bright
   [a] though spelled with *â*: **aimât**)
2. *a* when followed by silent final *s* (except in verb forms):
   pas [pɑ], **bas** [bɑ], **lilas** [lilɑ] (verbs ending in *-as* use
   bright [a]: **tu diras** [ty dira])
3. *a* when immediately followed by [s] (numerous exceptions):
   passer [pɑse], **classe** [klɑ:s(ə)], **basse** [bɑ:s(ə)], **hélas**
   [elɑs], **espace** [ɛspɑs(ə)]; some exceptions are: **chasser,**
   harasser, bassin, facile (use bright [a]).
4. *a* when followed by [z] (spelled with *-s-* or *-z-*):
   extase [ɛkstɑ:z(ə)], **gazon** [gɑzõ], **occasion** [ɔkɑzjõ],
   emphase [ãfɑ:z(ə)]

In addition, there are several isolated words that have dark [ɑ].
Dictionaries are not always in agreement about such words, but
some of them are:

diable [djɑ:bl(ə)]	**trois** [trwɑ]	**damner** [dɑne]
gars [gɑ]	**gagner** [gɑɲe]	**fable** [fɑ:bl(ə)]
paille [pɑ:j]	**cadavre** [kadɑ:vr(ə)]	

● [ɛ]

This symbol is used in English for the vowel in such words as *bed* and *get*. In the three languages discussed in this book, this sound is pronounced with a "higher" placement than in English. (See the discussion of this sound on p. 13.)

The many possible spellings of this sound in French are as follows:

- *è* (always): **mère, lève, arène, fidèle, paupière**
- *ê* (always): **tête, arrête, être, mêler**
- *ë*: **Noël, Israël** (except when silent in rare instances: **Saint-Saëns**)
- Medial *e* when followed by a consonant in the same syllable (except when nasalized) or a consonant cluster beginning with *s*:
  perdu [pɛrdy], **infernal** [ɛ̃fɛrnal], **bestiaire** [bɛstjɛːr(ə)]
- *e* when followed by a double consonant: **elle** [ɛl(ə)], **terre** [tɛːr(ə)], **guerre** [gɛːr(ə)], **cette** [sɛt], **tristesse** [tristɛs(ə)]
- *e* when followed by a final sounded consonant:
  mer [mɛːr], **avec** [avɛk], **bref** [brɛf], **quel** [kɛl]
- *e* followed by final silent *t*: **jet** [ʒɛ], **secret** [səkrɛ], **est** [ɛ], **cet** [sɛ], **effet** [efɛ], (exception: **et** [e])
- *e* in the words **les** [lɛ] **des** [dɛ] **ces** [sɛ] **mes** [mɛ] **ses** [sɛ] **tes** [tɛ] (spoken French uses [e] in these words, but sung French traditionally uses [ɛ])
- *ei* (except when nasalized): **neige** [nɛːʒ(ə)], **Seine** [sɛn(ə)], **pleine** [plɛn(ə)], **reine** [rɛn(ə)], including *e* before *-il* and *-ill*: **soleil** [sɔlɛːj], **abeille** [abɛːj(ə)], **veiller** [vɛje], and, rarely, *ey*: **Leguerney** [ləgɛrnɛ], **pleyon** [plɛjõ], **Pleyel** [plɛjɛl].
- *ai* (except when nasalized): **mais** [mɛ], **plaire** [plɛːr(ə)], **aime** [ɛm(ə)], **vrai** [vrɛ], **essai** [esɛ], including spelling variations *aie(s)*: **haie** [ɛ], **essaies** [esɛ], and verb endings *-ais*, *-ait*, *-aient*: **parlais** [parlɛ], **parlait** [parlɛ], **parlaient** [parlɛ]. Medial *ay* results in [ɛj] unless vocalic harmonization is applied: **payer** [pɛje] or [peje]. Final *-aye(s)* results in [ɛ]: **payes** [pɛ].

Exceptions to the above include:

- Initial *emm, enn* have [ɑ̃]: **emmener** [ɑ̃məne], **ennui** [ɑ̃nɥi], (**ennemi** however is [ɛnəmi]).
- Medial *emm, enn* have [a]: **femme** [fam(ə)], **solennel** [sɔlanɛl] (but **gemme** [ʒɛm(ə)], **flemme** [flɛm(ə)]).

- Initial *dess, desc, eff, ess* have [e]: **dessein** [desɛ̃], **dessert** [desɛ:r], **descendre** [desɑ̃:dr(ə)], **descriptif** [deskriptif], **effort** [efɔ:r], **effacer** [efase], **essaim** [esɛ̃], **essence** [esɑ̃s(ə)].
- Two *dess* words have [ə]: **dessous** [dəsu], **dessus** [dəsy].
- Initial *ress* usually has [ə]: **ressembler** [rəsɑ̃ble], **ressort** [rəsɔ:r], **ressource** [rəsurs(ə)].
- But two *ress* words have [e]: **ressuciter** [resysite], **ressuyer** [resɥije]. Also **pressentiment, pressentir, presser** have [pre...] but **presse, pressant have** [prɛ...].
- *-ail* and *-aill* result in [aj]: **corail** [kɔra:j], **travailler** [travaje]
- *-ai* is closed [e] when final in verb forms, which is usually first person singular of the future tense and *passé simple* (past historic tense): **parlerai** [parl(ə)re], **dirai** [dire], **verrai** [vɛre], **aimai** [eme], but also includes **j'ai** [ʒe]
- Some isolated words have *-ai* sounding as closed [e]: **je vais** [ʒə ve], **je sais** [ʒə se], **il sait** [il se], **gai** [ge], **quai** [ke]
- When *ai* is followed by a syllable with a closed vowel it may be [e] in some words: **aigu** [egy], **maison** [mezõ], **plaisir** [plezi:r] (see section on "Dictionaries," above)
- In the verb **faire** (to do, to make), the *-ai* is the normal open [ɛ] sound in most forms, but it is irregularly pronounced as schwa [ə] in two-syllable forms such as **faisons** [fəzõ], **faisant** [fəzɑ̃], **faisait** [fəzɛ]
- In situations calling for vocalic harmonization *-ai* may be [e]: **aimer** [eme]

● [e]

The closed [e] sound does not exist in standard English. The French and German versions of this sound are essentially identical (see p. 72). It is very closed and is almost in the position of [i]. English-speaking singers unused to this sound tend to pronounce and sing it closer to the position of [ɛ]. It is recommended that the novice substitute [i] in situations calling for [e] in the presence of a coach or teacher, who can guide the singer in finding the appropriate shape.

The spelling of this sound in French is as follows:

- *é* (always): **étoile** [etwal(ə)], **volupté** [vɔlypte], **légère** [leʒɛ:r(ə)], **été** [ete]
- *e* (when not nasalized) before final silent consonants except *s* and *t*: **pied** [pje], **clef** [kle], **chez** [ʃe], **nez** [ne], including all verb forms ending in *-er* and *-ez*: **parler** [parle], **parlez**

[parle], **aimer** [eme], **aimez** [eme], **disiez** [dizje], as well as polysyllabic nouns/adjectives ending in *-er*:
boulanger [bulɑ̃ʒe], **charpentier** [ʃarpɑ̃tje], **février** [fevrje], **léger** [leʒe], **baiser** [beze] (monosyllables and a few polysyllables ending in *-er* have [ɛr] as in **mer, cher, hiver**)

- *e* in initial *dess-* and *desc-*: **dessein** [desɛ̃], **dessécher** [deseʃe], **descendre** [desɑ̃dr(ə)] (except for two words: **dessous** [dəsu] and **dessus** [dəsy])
- *e* in initial *eff-* and *ess-*: **effet** [efɛ], **effort** [efɔːr], **effaroucher** [efaruʃe], **effroi** [efrwa], **essor** [esɔːr], **essuyer** [esɥije] and in some words with initial *ress-* and *press-*: **ressusciter** [resysite], **ressuyer** [resɥije], **pressentir** [presɑ̃tiːr]
- *ai* when final in verb forms, usually first person singular of the future tense and *passé simple* (past historic tense): **serai** [səre], **j'irai** [ʒire], **ferai** [fəre], **donnai** [dɔne]; also **j'ai** [ʒe] and, irregularly: **je vais** [ʒə ve], **je sais** [ʒə se], **il sait** [il se]
- *ai* when the following syllable has a closed vowel (see section on "Dictionaries"): **plaisir** [pleziːr], **maison** [mezõ], **aigu** [egy]
- *ai* in some isolated words: **quai** [ke], **gai** [ge] (and derivatives)
- *ay* in **pays** [pei] and derivatives **paysage** [peizaːʒ(ə)], **paysan** [peizɑ̃], and in vocalic harmonization: **payer** [pɛje] or [peje], **baiser** [bɛze] or [beze]

● **[ɔ]**

The open sound [ɔ] is the same sound encountered in Italian (**cosa**), German (**Sonne**), British English (**hot**), and American English (**awe**). In some French words the shortness of the vowel sound results in a quality almost approaching that of English [ʌ], though rounder: **comme, bonne, donner.**

The spelling of [ɔ] in French is as follows:

- *o* when followed by a sounded consonant or *h* in the same word (except the sound [z], see p. 130) or another vowel-letter sounding as a separate vowel sound in the same word:

dormir [dɔrmiːr]	**frivole** [frivɔl(ə)]	**soleil** [sɔlɛːj]
joli [ʒɔli]	**donner** [dɔne]	**poète** [pɔɛt(ə)]
Noël [nɔɛl]	**bohème** [bɔɛm(ə)]	

(Final *o* or *o* plus a final silent consonant results in [o]. See next section.) *Most of the time, therefore, the letter* o *will re-*

sult in open [ɔ] when it is the only vowel-letter in the syllable and is not nasalized (see below for individual exceptions).

- *au* only when followed by *r*: **Fauré** [fɔre], **aurore** [ɔrɔr(ə)], **saurais** [sɔrɛ], and in two isolated words: **mauvais** [mɔvɛ], **Paul** [pɔl]. Otherwise *au* results in [o]. See below.

● [o]

The closed sound [o] is equivalent to German [o] (**Sohn**). It is not normally used in English. It is analogous to [e] in that it is very closed, close to the position of [u].

The spelling of [o] in French is as follows:

- *o* when final in a word: **écho** [eko], **Roméo** [rɔmeo]
- *o* when followed by a final silent consonant:
  mot [mo], **trop** [tro], **éclos** [eklo]
- *o* when followed by the sound [z] (spelled *s* or *z*):
  rose [ro:z(ə)], **chose** [ʃo:z(ə)]
- *ô* (always): **hôtel** [otɛl], **hôpital** [opital], **geôlier** [ʒolje]
- *au* usually (except before *r*, see above: **automne** [otɔn(ə)], **autre** [otr(ə)], **faux** [fo]
- *eau* (always): **l'eau** [lo], **beau** [bo], **anneau** [ano], **oiseau** [wazo]
- Isolated exceptions having [o]: **odeur** [odœ:r], **grosse** [gros(ə)], **fosse** [fos(ə)], **vomir** [vomi:r], **émotion** [emosjõ]

● [i]

The sound [i] is the same as in English **see**. In French [i] is spelled:

- *i, î*, or *ï*, when the only vowel-letter in the syllable and not nasalized: **ici** [isi], **île** [il(ə)], **haïr** [air]
- *y* or *ÿ* when the only vowel-letter in the syllable and not nasalized: **cygne** [siɲ(ə)], **lys** [lis], **Louÿs** [lwis]

In spoken French, final *-ie* is [i]: vie [vi], mélancolie [melãkɔli]. Usually musical settings give a separate note for the final *e* in a combination of *ie*; it is then pronounced [iə]:

Lydia (Fauré)

rends - moi___ la **vi** - e
[rã mwa la viə]

If there is no separate note for the mute [ə] the combination is sung as [i]:

Soupir (Debussy)

où   la fauve **a - go - nie** Des   feuil - les
[u la fo:v agɔni dɛ fœ:jə]

When *-ie* ends a syllable within a word (medially) it is always just [i]. This happens in forms of verbs whose infinitives end in *-ier*. The infinitive has [ie] as in **oublier** [ublie], **prier** [prie] (some dictionaries give [ije] for these words), but in other forms the medial *ie* is [i] only:

Chanson triste (Duparc)

J'ou - blie - rai   les   dou-leurs pas (sées)
[ʒublire lɛ dulœ:r pase]

Faust

Non!___   tu ne **prie-ras** pas!___
[nõ ty nə prira pɑ]

Carmen

qui nous **li - e** nous **lie - ra** jus- qu'au tré - pas
[ki nu liə nu lira ʒysko trepɑ]

When *-ie* is followed by another letter in the syllable, however, it will be [ie] as in verb infinitives discussed above, or [jɛ]: **hier** [jɛr], **miel** [mjɛl].

● **[u]**

The sound [u] is the same as English **do**, but without the diphthong glide-off. It is the same as Italian **tu** and German **du**. (See p. 10 for a discussion of this sound.)

In French [u] is spelled: *ou* and variations *où, oû, aou, aoû:*

toujours [tuʒuːr]   **coût** [ku]   **doux** [du]
retour [rətuːr]   **août** [u]   **saoul** [su]

When *ou* is followed by another vowel in the same syllable, it usually acts as the glide [w]:

ouest [wɛst] **oui** [wi] **rouage** [rwaʒ(ə)] **rouet** [rwɛ] **jouer** [ʒwe]

However, musical settings of such words often turn the glide into a vowel (see "Glides").

    ou followed by *ill* results in [uj]: **ouiller** [uje], **brouillard** [brujaːr].

    When the combination *oue* is final in a word it is pronounced [u], but composers will often set the mute *e* on a separate note, requiring it to be pronounced as schwa [ə].

    When the same combination *oue* is medial (most commonly in verb forms), it is always just [u]: **rouerie** [ruri], **jouerai** [ʒure].

Carmen

et   nous **jouer- ons**   la bel - le
[e nu ʒurõ la bɛl(ə)]

    Remember that when *-oue* is followed by another consonant in the same syllable, the *e* is no longer mute: **rouet** [rwɛ], **jouer** [ʒwe] (see "Glides").

● **[y]**

This "mixed" vowel sound is the same as the German closed sound spelled with *ü* as in **müde**. The key to this sound is the arched tongue position of [i]. Students unfamiliar with French see the vowel-letter *u* and instinctively want to pronounce [u]. The lips round to an [u] position, but the tongue must remain arched as for [i]. Some modification is called for in the high voice, of course.

    In French this sound is spelled as follows:

• *u, û*, when the only vowel-letter in the syllable and not nasalized: **une** [yn(ə)], **sur** [syr], **brûle** [bryl(ə)], **rendu** [rãdy], **dessus** [dəsy].

Final *-ue(s)* is usually set with two notes as [yə]:

Après un rêve (Fauré)

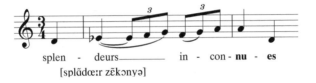

splen - deurs_____ in - con - **nu** - **es**
[splɑ̃dœːr zɛ̃kɔnyə]

but is sometimes set on one note as [y]

La pintade (Ravel)

C'est la **bos-sue** de ma cour
[sɛ la bɔsy də ma kuːr]

Medial *ue* divides [yɛ] after consonant plus *l* or *r*: **cruel** [kryɛl], **fluet** [flyɛ], but *u* following *g* or *q* is usually silent: **guerre** [gɛːr(ə)], **que** [kə].

Verb infinitives in -*uer* have [ɥe]: **muer** [mɥe], **tuer** [tɥe], but musical settings usually change the glide to a vowel ([mye], [tye]). Other forms of these verbs have a mute *e* which is always silent, even in singing: **muera** [myra], **tuera** [tyra].

When *u* precedes other vowel-letters, it usually functions as the glide [ɥ]: **nuit** [nɥi]. (See "Glides.")

• *eu, eû*, only in forms of the verb **avoir** (normally *eu* is [œ] or [ø]):

j'ai eu [je y]   **il eut** [il y]   **nous eûmes** [nu zym(ə)]

La Damnation de Faust

que   s'il **eût**   **eu**   l'a - mour au   corps
[kə sil y ty lamuːr o kɔːr]

● [œ]

This mixed vowel sound is the same as the German open sound spelled with *ö* as in **Götter**. The tongue and jaw are positioned for [ɛ] and the lips round to [ɔ].

In French this sound is spelled as follows:

- *eu* and variations *oeu, ueu,* when followed by a pronounced consonant-letter or by *-il, -ill*:

fleur [flœ:r]	**seul** [sœl]	**neuf** [nœf]
coeur [kœ:r]	**oeuf** [œf]	**soeur** [sœ:r]
langueur [lɑ̃gœ:r]	**vainqueur** [vɛ̃kœ:r]	**feuille** [fœ:j(ə)]
deuil [dœ:j]		

(Note that *ueu* only happens after *g* and *q,* and the first *u* is silent.) Exceptions: words ending in *-euse* take [ø], as do the few words ending in *-eutre* and *-eute.* See next section.
- *ue* in forms *cueil* and *gueil*: **cueillir** [kœji:r], **orgueil** [ɔrgœ:j]
- *oe* in forms *oeil*: **oeil** [œ:j], **oeillet** [œjɛ].

Remember that this sound is subject to vocalic harmonization: **heureux** [œrø] or [ørø].

● [ø]

The sound [ø] is the same as the German closed sound spelled with *ö* as in **böse.** The tongue and jaw are positioned for [e] and the lips round to [o]. As always with mixed vowels, the tongue position is of primary importance.

The French spelling of this sound is *eu* and variations *oeu, ueu,* when final in a word or followed by a final silent consonant:

feu [fø]	**peu** [pø]	**dieu** [djø]
pleut [plø]	**aïeux** [ajø]	**voeu** [vø]
oeufs [ø]	**fougueux** [fugø]	**queue** [kø]

The common feminine ending *-euse* is pronounced [ø:z(ə)]:

radieuse [radjø:z(ə)] **amoureuse** [amurø:z(ə)] **chanteuse** [ʃɑ̃tø:z(ə)]

The rare forms with *-eutre* and *-eute* also use [ø]: **neutre** [nøtr(ə)], **meute** [møt(ə)], and also the isolated word **jeûne** [ʒø:n(ə)].

● Breakdown of Mixed Vowels

The following chart is useful in remembering how the mixed vowels are formulated. This information is essential for the singer and should be memorized.

Tongue/jaw position of [i] plus lip position of [u] = [y]
Tongue/jaw position of [e] plus lip position of [o] = [ø]
Tongue/jaw position of [ɛ] plus lip position of [ɔ] = [œ]

Remember that the core of the mixed vowel sound is the tongue position. If any problem is encountered with a mixed vowel, reduce it to the vowel of the tongue position only. See p. 79 for a somewhat different version of this chart.

● [ə]

The symbol [ə] is called schwa. It represents a short, unstressed, neutral vowel sound. It is used in IPA for any language that employs such a sound, including German and English. When such a sound is lengthened for singing, the vowel quality varies from language to language. In French the schwa symbol is used for mute *e*, and the sound is generally considered to be the same as [œ] when it is sustained for singing, although depending on context (e.g., before or after a closed vowel), it may close somewhat. It will definitely close to [ø] in vocalic harmonization.

In French the schwa [ə] is used in IPA transcriptions whenever the vowel-letter *e*, without accent, is the only vowel-letter in the syllable, and is either final or (when medial) precedes a consonant plus a vowel (see "Syllabification"). When unaccented *e* ends a syllable following *gu* and *qu*, it is also schwa. Parentheses around the schwa [(ə)] indicate that this sound is generally silent in speech but pronounced in singing. Examples:

- Final in monosyllables:

  de [də] **le** [lə] **me** [mə] **te** [tə] **ne** [nə] **que** [kə] **se** [sə]

- Final in polysyllabic words (silent in spoken French):

  bague [bag(ə)]   **aime** [ɛm(ə)]   **fille** [fij(ə)]
  cette [sɛt(ə)]   **mystère** [mistɛ:r(ə)]

- Preceding a consonant plus a vowel (medial) (also generally silent in spoken French):

  reviens [rəvjɛ̃]   **cheval** [ʃ(ə)val]
  médecin [med(ə)sɛ̃]   **parlerai** [parl(ə)re]
  querelle [kərɛl(ə)]   **souvenir** [suv(ə)n:ir]
  Marguerite [marg(ə)rit(ə)]

- Final *-es* in plural forms of nouns and adjectives (but not monosyllables like **les**) and in verb endings (silent in spoken French):

  courtes vestes [kurt(ə) vɛst(ə)]   **jeunes filles** [ʒœn(ə) fi:j(ə)]
  tu parles [ty parl(ə)]

- Final *-ent* in verb endings of the third person plural, present tense (silent in spoken French):

  ils aiment [il zɛm(ə)]   **ils viennent** [il vjɛn(ə)]
  ils parlent [il parl(ə)]

  Remember that the *-aient* ending (imperfect tense) is [ɛ] only:

  ils aimaient [il zɛmɛ]   **ils accouraient** [il zakurɛ]
  ils disaient [il dizɛ]

  Remember that when *-ent* is not a verb ending, it is [ɑ̃]:
  souvent [suvɑ̃], **comment** [kɔmɑ̃], **maintenent** [mɛ̃t(ə)nɑ̃].
- *ai* in forms of the verb **faire**, when ai precedes s [z]:

  faisons [fəzõ],   **faisant** [fəzɑ̃],   **faisait** [fəzɛ]

  (See p. 160 for a complete discussion of musical settings of schwa.)

● Nasal Vowels—General

French has four nasal vowels: [ɑ̃], [ɛ̃], [õ], [œ̃]. All four sounds occur in the phrase **un bon vin blanc** [œ̃ bõ vɛ̃ blɑ̃]. The nasal quality of the vowels should be light, unexaggerated.

The pattern for determining nasalization of a vowel is consistent for all of them:

*A vowel will be nasalized if it is followed by **n** or **m** in the same syllable. The **n** or **m** is not in the same syllable if it is immediately followed by a vowel, **m**, **n**, or **h** in the same word.*

Examples of words with nasal vowels (*n* or *m* part of the same syllable as the preceding vowel):

vain [vɛ̃]	**enfant** [ɑ̃fɑ̃]	**ingrat** [ɛ̃gra]
humble [œ̃:bl(ə)]	**dompter** [dõte]	**ombrage** [õbra:ʒ(ə)]
bientôt [bjɛ̃to]	**printemps** [prɛ̃tɑ̃]	**un** [œ̃]

Examples of words without nasal vowels (*n* or *m* in a different syllable from the preceding vowel):

vaine [vɛn(ə)]	**bonheur** [bɔnœ:r]
automne [otɔn(ə)]	**tenir** [təni:r]
anneau [ano]	**inégal** [inegal]
immémoriale [imemɔrjal(ə)]	**une** [yn(ə)]

The *n* or *m* in the syllable of the nasal vowel is not pronounced except when a final *n* is in liaison. (See "Liaison.")

Exceptions to the nasalization rule are limited to words beginning with *en*, *enn*, and *(r)emm*:

enamourer [ɑ̃namure] **enorgueiller** [ɑ̃nɔrgœje]
enivrer [ɑ̃nivre] **ennui** [ɑ̃nɥi]
ennoblir [ɑ̃nɔbli:r] **emmener** [ɑ̃m(ə)ne]
emmeler [ɑ̃m(ə)le] **remmener** [rɑ̃m(ə)ne]

A single *enn-* word is *not* nasalized: **ennemi** [ɛnəmi].

When *n* precedes *d* or *t* there is a particular tendency to pronounce the *n*, because the tongue is in the same position for all three sounds. Pronounce:

onde [õ:d(ə)] **intime** [ɛ̃tim(ə)]
candeur [kɑ̃dœ:r] **monter** [mõte]
lamente [lamɑ̃:t(ə)] **plainte dormante** [plɛ̃:t(ə) dɔrmɑ̃:t(ə)]

Similarly, when *m* precedes *b* or *p*, there is a greater tendency to pronounce the *m* because the lips are closed for all three sounds: Pronounce:

ombre [õ:br(ə)] **impossible** [ɛ̃pɔsibl(ə)] **embarquer** [ɑ̃barke]

When a nasal vowel precedes the sounds [k] or [g] there is a tendency for English speakers to pronounce [ŋ], since that is what happens in English. The sound [ŋ] does not exist in French.

anglais [ɑ̃glɛ] *not* [ɑ̃ŋglɛ] **encore** [ɑ̃kɔ:r(ə)] *not* [ɑ̃ŋkɔ:r(ə)]
oncle [õ:kl(ə)] *not* [õ:ŋkl(ə)] **fringant** [frɛ̃gɑ̃] *not* [frɛ̃ŋgɑ̃]

● [ɑ̃]

As the IPA symbol implies, it is the dark version of the vowel that is nasalized. Though it is dark, it is open; otherwise it could be confused with [õ].

The spelling of this sound in French is as follows:

• *an*: **chant** [ʃɑ̃], **antan** [ɑ̃tɑ̃], **danser** [dɑ̃se]
• *am*: **champ** [ʃɑ̃], **flambeau** [flɑ̃bo], **Samson** [sɑ̃sõ]
• *en*: **enfer** [ɑ̃fɛr], **serment** [sɛrmɑ̃], **splendeur** [splɑ̃dœ:r]
• *em*: **temps** [tɑ̃], **semble** [sɑ̃:bl(ə)], **emplir** [ɑ̃pli:r]

Exceptions: Words ending in *-ien* and *-en* have [jɛ̃]: **bien** [bjɛ̃], **chien** [ʃjɛ̃], **chrétien** [kretjɛ̃], **examen** [ɛgzamɛ̃], as do verb endings *-iens, -ient*: **viens** [vjɛ̃], **tient** [tjɛ̃]; but these words have [jɑ̃]: **patient** [pasjɑ̃], **patience** [pasjɑ̃:s(ə)]. The name **Poulenc** is [pulɛ̃:k].

Other exceptions are final *-yen*: **Troyen** [trwajɛ̃], **moyen** [mwajɛ̃], and some proper names: **Jonathan** [ʒɔnatan].

Less common variations of the principal spellings are:

- *aen*: **Messiaen** [mɛsjɑ̃], **Caen** [kɑ̃]
- *aën*: **Saint-Saëns** [sɛ̃ sɑ̃:s]
- *ean*: **Jean** [ʒɑ̃]
- *aon*: **paon** [pɑ̃]

● [ɛ̃]

This is the one nasal vowel in which the original vowel shape changes slightly in the nasal version. When nasalized, the original open [ɛ] position is "tilted" forward. This can be accomplished by gently rounding the lips, or by gently shaping the vowel <u>in the direction of</u> [æ] as in English **hat**. Do not exaggerate, however!

The spelling of this sound in French is as follows:

- *in*: **vin** [vɛ̃], **Marin** [marɛ̃], **insensé** [ɛ̃sɑ̃se]
- *im*: **timbre** [tɛ̃:br(ə)], **important** [ɛ̃pɔrtɑ̃]
- *yn*: **lynx** [lɛ̃:ks], **syncope** [sɛ̃kɔp(ə)]
- *ym*: **thym** [tɛ̃], **symphonie** [sɛ̃fɔni]

Variations of the above are:

- *ain*: **pain** [pɛ̃], **certain** [sɛrtɛ̃], **ainsi** [ɛ̃si]
- *aim*: **faim** [fɛ̃], **daim** [dɛ̃]
- *ein*: **ceinture** [sɛ̃ty:r(ə)], **plein** [plɛ̃]
- *eim*: **Reims** [rɛ̃:s]
- Final *-ien* is [jɛ̃]: **ancien** [ɑ̃sjɛ̃], **rien** [rjɛ̃], **mien** [mjɛ̃]
- Final *-yen*: **moyen** [mwajɛ̃], **Troyen** [trwajɛ̃], **doyen** [dwajɛ̃]
- Verb endings with *-ien-* in verbs like **venir** and **tenir**: **je tiens** [ʒə tjɛ̃], **elle vient** [ɛl(ə) vjɛ̃], **il viendra** [il vjɛ̃dra]
- Final *-en* (rare): **examen** [ɛgzamɛ̃]
- Some proper names such as **Poulenc** [pulɛ̃:k]
- *-oin* is [wɛ̃]: **loin** [lwɛ̃], **besoin** [bəzwɛ̃], **point** [pwɛ̃], **poing** [pwɛ̃]

● [õ]

The sound [õ] was originally rendered as [ɔ̃] in IPA. In recent years the accepted symbol has become [õ]. This is more appropriate since it is the closed version of the vowel that is nasalized. Of the four nasal vowels this is the only one that is closed.

The spelling of this sound in French is as follows:

- *on*: **bon** [bõ], **fontaine** [fõtɛn(ə)], **vont** [võ], **voyons** [vwajõ]
- *om*: **nom** [nõ], **tomber** [tõbe], **rompre** [rõːpr(ə)]

● [œ̃]

The sound [œ̃] is the most difficult for students to get right. There are two ways to find it:

1. The usual way is to isolate the vowel [œ] and then to add nasal quality. Unfortunately, students tend to change the [œ] sound when nasality is added.
2. An alternative is to isolate the nasal vowel [ɛ̃], which is usually not a difficult sound for students to make, then round the lips while keeping the jaw open.

Students who have trouble with this sound tend to substitute [ɑ̃]. In such cases it is advisable to substitute [ɛ̃] as the nearest sound. If this habit can be trained, rounding of the lips for the true [œ̃] is not difficult.

The spelling of this sound in French is as follows:

- *un*: **un** [œ̃], **lundi** [lœ̃di], **brun** [brœ̃], **Verdun** [vɛrdœ̃], **opportun** [ɔpɔrtœ̃]
- *um*: **parfum** [parfœ̃], **humble** [œ̃ːbl(ə)]

Glides

A glide is a very short vowel sound that gives way immediately to the primary vowel sound of the syllable. French has three glides: [j], [w], and [ɥ]. (See p. 167 for musical settings of glides.)

● [j]

[j] is a short, rapid [i]. This glide can be spelled as follows:

- *i* when followed by a vowel other than [ə]: **ciel** [sjɛl], **précieux** [presjø], **science** [sjɑ̃ːs(ə)] (remember that words with *ie* after consonant plus *l* or *r* have no glide): **prier** [prie], **oublier** [ublie]
- *ï* and *y*: **aïeux** [ajø], **payer** [peje], **royal** [rwajal], **yeux** [jø]

- *ill* following a vowel is [j]:

abeille [abɛːj(ə)]	**feuillage** [fœjaːʒ(ə)]
travailler [travaje]	**cueillir** [kœjiːr]
ailleurs [ajœːr]	**cailloux** [kaju]
oeillet [œjɛ]	**mouiller** [muje]

- *ill* following a consonant is [iːj]: **fille** [fiːj(ə)], **famille** [famiːj(ə)] Exceptions: three words and their derivatives: **mille** [mil(ə)], **ville** [vil(ə)], **tranquille** [trãkil(ə)], and initial *ill*: **illusion** [ilyzjõ], **illumination** [ilyminasjõ]
- In a few proper names the combination *lh* results in the [j] glide:
  Milhaud [mijo], **Paladilhe** [paladiːj(ə)], **Carvalho** [karvajo]
- final *-il* and *-ilh* after a vowel are [j] though technically not glides:
  soleil [sɔlɛːj], **corail** [kɔraːj], **cercueil** [sɛrkœːj], **Anouilh** [anuːj]

The combination *-ti-* is pronounced [sj] in certain suffixes:

- *-tion*: **addition** [adisjõ], **motion** [mɔsjõ], but not after *s*: **question** [kɛstjõ] or in verbs: **sortions** [sɔrtjõ]
- *-tience*: **patience** (pasjãːs(ə))
- *-tient(e)*: **patient** [pasjã], **patiente** [pasjãːt(ə)]
- *-tien(ne)*: **vénitien** [venisjɛ̃], **vénitienne** [venisjɛn(ə)]
- *-tiel(le)*: **confidentiel** [kõfidãsjɛl], **essentielle** [esãsjɛl(ə)]
- *-tieux(se)*: **ambitieux** [ãbisjø], **minutieuse** [minysjøːz(ə)]
- *-tiable*: **insatiable** [ɛ̃sasjabl(ə)]

Some words with *ti* have [tj], including some *-tien(ne)* words:

chrétien [kretjɛ̃]   **antienne** [ãtjɛn(ə)]   **entretien** [ãtr(ə)tjɛ̃]

● [w]

[w] is a short, rapid, [u]. This glide can be spelled as follows:

- *ou* followed by a vowel other than mute *e*: **oui** [wi], **ouest** [wɛst], **jouer** [ʒwe] Exception: *ou* followed by *ill* is [uj]: **mouillé** [muje], **brouillé** [bruje].
- *oi* results in [wa] or [wɑ]:

foi [fwa]	**roi** [rwa]	**sois** [swa]
vois [vwa]	**noir** [nwaːr]	**oiseau** [wazo]
soif [swaf]	**croire** [krwɑːr(ə)]	**effroi** [efrwɑ]

- Final *oie* is [wa]: **soie** [swa], **joie** [ʒwa]; or [waə] if the *e* is given its own note; medial *oie* is always [wa]: **soient** [swa].

- *oin* results in [wɛ̃]: **besoin** [bəzwɛ̃], **loin** [lwɛ̃], **moindre** [mwɛ̃:dr(ə)]. *oy* followed by another vowel results in [waj]: **voyage** [vwaja:ʒ(ə)], **voyez** [vwaje], **loyal** [lwajal], **moyen** [mwajɛ̃], **foyer** [fwaje].

● [ɥ]

Unlike [w] and [j], the glide [ɥ] does not occur in English. For this reason it is often a difficult sound for the student to acquire. When it is incorrect it sounds like [w]; **nuit** is pronounced [nwi]. One way to solve this problem is to have the student shape the lips for [y] <u>as the preceding consonant is being articulated</u>. If the shaping of the lips happens after the consonant, it is too late and [w] will result.

[ɥ] is a short, rapid [y]. It is spelled only with *u* followed by a vowel other than mute *e*:

nuit [nɥi]	**lui** [lɥi]	**suis** [sɥi]
fui [fɥi]	**fruit** [frɥi]	**Juif** [ʒɥif]
cuisine [kɥizin(ə)]	**suave** [sɥa:v(ə)]	**nuage** [nɥa:ʒ(ə)]
muet [mɥɛ]		

Exceptions: when *u* follows *g* or *q* it is usually silent:

languir [lɑ̃gi:r]	**guetter** [gɛte]	**Guy** [gi]
muguet [mygɛ]	**qui** [ki]	**que** [kə]
quatre [katr(ə)]	**quasi** [kazi]	**question** [kɛstjõ]

The word **aiguille** and derivatives have [gɥi]—[egɥi:j(ə)]).
A few words have *qu* as [kw]:

quatuor [kwatɥɔ:r]   **adéquat** [adekwa]   **aquarelle** [akwarɛl(ə)]

The pattern consonant plus *l* or *r* preceding *ua, ue,* or *ui* results in a vowel instead of a glide:
cruel [kryɛl], **cruauté** [kryote], **fluide** [flyid(ə)].

uy results in [ɥij]: **fuyez** [fɥije] **essuyage** [esɥija:ʒ(ə)] **ennuyer** [ɑ̃nɥije]. In the word **bruyère**, the consonant plus *r* pattern results in [bryjɛ:r(ə)] (no [ɥ] glide).

Consonants

Any discussion of French consonants must make a distinction between consonant sounds and consonant-letters, since the letters are often silent. Individual consonant-letters as well as combinations are presented in alphabetical order, with an explanation of their sounds and when they are silent. To facilitate this, the discussion of each letter is in two general parts:

1. When the letter ends a word
2. When the letter is initial or medial in a word

The reason for this is that final consonant-letters are usually silent, whereas consonant-letters elsewhere in a word are usually sounded.

Knowing when final consonants are sounded or silent is one of the more difficult aspects about learning French pronunciation. A helpful device is the so-called rule of "careful." The four consonant-letters in this English word are usually sounded when found at the end of a French word, while all other consonant-letters are usually silent when at the end of a French word. Useful as this crutch is, there are numerous exceptions.

Any consonant before final mute *e* is pronounced. Many French words have masculine forms ending in a silent letter and feminine forms that add a mute *e*, causing the preceding consonant to be pronounced:

> **froid** [fʀwa] **froide** [fʀwad(ə)] **vain** [vɛ̃] **vaine** [vɛːn(ə)]
> **Jean** [ʒɑ̃] **Jeanne** [ʒɑn(ə)] **berger** [bɛʀʒe] **bergère** [bɛʀʒɛːr(ə)]

Remember that double consonants in French are not lengthened in the Italian manner, except for initial *ill-*, *imm-*, *inn-*, and *irr-*.

The following pages discuss the sounds of French consonants and consonant combinations in alphabetical order.

Consonants in Detail

● **B**

When Final

Final *b* is rare in French. If it follows a nasal vowel it is silent, as in **plomb** [plõ]. It is sounded at the end of proper names: **Mab** [mab], **Jacob** [ʒakɔb].

Initial/medial

b and *bb* sound as [b]: **bouche** [buʃ(ə)], **abbé** [abe], except preceding an unvoiced consonant, when it is [p]:

obtenir [ɔpt(ə)niːr] **absence** [apsɑ̃s(ə)] **obscur** [ɔpskyːr]
observer [ɔpsɛrve]

● C, Ç, CC

When Final

As one of the "careful" consonants, *c* is usually sounded as [k] when final in French words:

arc [ark]   **parc** [park]   **turc** [tyrk]   **lac** [lak]   **sec** [sɛk]   **bec** [bɛk]

including proper names:

Duparc [dypark]   **Bernac** [bɛrnak]   **Poulenc** [pulɛ̃:k]

In spite of "Poulenc," *c* is usually silent when preceded by a nasal vowel:

banc [bɑ̃]   **jonc** [ʒɔ̃]   **franc** [frɑ̃]

and silent in a few individual words:

estomac [ɛstɔma]   **tabac** [taba]   **croc** [cro]

The word **donc** is somewhat confusing. Most dictionaries give [dɔ̃:k], but in practice it is often pronounced [dɔ̃]. French pronunciation books are not in total agreement, but the majority consensus is as follows:
It is pronounced [dɔ̃:k]

1. At the beginning of a sentence or clause when its meaning is "therefore":

   je pense, donc [dɔ̃:k] **je suis.**
   Donc, ce sera par un clair jour d'été. [dɔ̃:k sə səra . . .]

2. In liaison:

   Il est donc [dɔ̃:k] **entendu que . . .**
   Mais où donc est l'amour? [mɛ u dɔ̃ kɛ lamu:r]

3. When standing alone as an interjection: **Donc!** [dɔ̃:k]

Otherwise it is pronounced [dɔ̃]:

qu'as tu donc?
Il est donc venu.

Initial/Medial

As in other languages, the letter *c* has two sounds in French:

1. "Hard" *c* is pronounced [k] and occurs when *c* is followed by *a*, *o*, *u*, or a consonant: **carte** [kart(ə)], **comme** [kɔm(ə)], **vaincu** [vɛ̃ky], **écrire** [ekri:r(ə)].
   The word **second** and derivatives irregularly have [g]: [səgɔ̃].
   Final *-ct* is silent in **aspect** [aspɛ], otherwise it is sounded: **direct** [dirɛkt], **exact** [egzact].
2. "Soft" *c* is pronounced [s] and occurs when *c* is followed by *e*, *i*, or *y*: **facile** [fasil(ə)], **cette** [sɛt(ə)], **ceci** [səsi], **ciel** [sjɛl], **cygne** [siɲ(ə)], including the combinations *sce* and *sci*: **ascenseur** [asɑ̃sœ:r], **scintiller** [sɛ̃tije].

The letter *ç* is always pronounced [s]. It is used in a few words to create [s] before *a*, *o*, or *u*:

ça [sa]   **leçon** [ləsɔ̃]   **garçon** [garsɔ̃]   **aperçu** [apɛrsy]

Double *cc* is [k] when followed by *a*, *o*, *u*, or a consonant:

acclamer [aklame]   **occuper** [ɔkype]   **raccord** [rakɔ:r]

Double *cc* is [ks] when followed by *e* or *i*: **accident** [aksidɑ̃], **accepter** [aksɛpte]. (Note how this is similar to English but different from Italian.)

● CH

The combination *ch* is usually pronounced [ʃ]. This is the only way to spell this sound in French. The French version is pronounced with more lip rounding than the English version.

chercher [ʃɛrʃe]   **achever** [aʃ(ə)ve]   **fiche** [fiʃ(ə)]   **boucher** [buʃe]

In words of Greek origin, *ch* is pronounced [k]:

choeur [kœ:r]   **orchestre** [orkɛstr(ə)]   **chrétien** [kretjɛ̃]   **écho** [eko]

● D

As in Italian, the sound [d] is never aspirated (released with a puff of air) in French, as it is in English and German. It must be pronounced dentally, that is, the tongue making contact with the back of the upper front teeth.

When Final

Usually final *d* is silent:

froid [frwa]   **pied** [pje]   **quand** [kɑ̃]   **canard** [kana:r]

It is sounded in proper names:

le Cid [sid]   **Alfred** [alfrɛd]   **Yniold** [injɔld]

and in the isolated word **sud** [syd].

In liaison, *d* sounds as [t] (see "Liaison"): **quand‿il** [kɑ̃ til].

Initial/Medial

d and *dd* sound as [d]:

dans [dɑ̃]   **fidèle** [fidɛ:l(ə)]   **addition** [adisjɔ̃]

● F

When Final

As one of the "careful" consonants, *f* is usually pronounced as [f] when final in French words:

chef [ʃɛf]   **soif** [swaf]   **if** [if]   **bref** [brɛf]   **furtif** [fyrtif]

A few words have silent final *f*:

clef [kle]   **nerf** [nɛ:r]   **cerf** [sɛ:r]   **chef-d'oeuvres** [ʃɛ dœ:vr(ə)]

The words **oeuf** [œf] and **boeuf** [bœf] are irregular in the pronunciation of their plurals: **oeufs** [ø] and **boeufs** [bø].

In two phrases *f* sounds as [v]: **neuf heures** [nœvœr(ə)] and **neuf ans** [nœvɑ̃]. This is not liaison, since *f* is already pronounced in **neuf**.

Initial/Medial

f and *ff* always sound as [f]: **fin** [fɛ̃], **affaire** [afɛ:r(ə)]

● G, GG

When Final

When *g* ends a French word it normally follows a nasal vowel and is silent:

sang [sɑ̃]   **poing** [pwɛ̃]   **long** [lɔ̃]   also **bourg** [bu:r]

Final *g* in liaison sounds as [k] (see "Liaison"): **long‿hiver** [lɔ̃kivɛ:r].

Initial/Medial

As in other languages, *g* has two sounds:

1. "Hard" *g* and *gg* are pronounced [g], occurring when they are followed by *a, o, u,* or another consonant: **gauche** [go:ʃ(ə)], **goûter** [gute], **aggraver** [agrave], **figure** [figy:r(ə)]
2. "Soft" *g* is [ʒ] as in the English word "pleasure" [plɛʒɚ] and occurs when *g* is followed by *e, i,* or *y*: **givre** [ʒi:vr(ə)], **rouge** [ru:ʒ(ə)], **gymnaste** [ʒimnast(ə)]

Note: Whenever *gu* is followed by a vowel, the *u* has no phonetic value of its own (that is, it is not [y] or [ɥ]). Its only purpose is to render the *g* hard:

guerre [gɛ:r(ə)]   **languir** [lɑ̃gi:r]   **guide** [gid(ə)]   **baguette** [bagɛt(ə)]

Similarly, whenever *ge* is followed by another vowel, the *e* is unphonetic, serving only to render the *g* soft:

nageais [naʒɛ]   **songeait** [sɔ̃ʒɛ]   **changea** [ʃɑ̃ʒa]   **Georges** [ʒɔ:rʒ(ə)]

When double *gg* is followed by *e* or *é* it is [gʒ]: **suggérer** [sygʒere], **suggestion** [sygʒɛstjɔ̃].

● GN

As in Italian, the combination *gn* is normally pronounced [ɲ]:

ignoble [iɲɔbl(ə)]	**baigner** [beɲe]	**agneau** [aɲo]
cygne [siɲ(ə)]	**rogner** [rɔɲe]	

See p. 29 for a discussion of this sound. Exception: **stagnant, stagnante** [stagnɑ̃] [stagnɑ̃:t(ə)].

There is no [ʎ] sound in French, so *gl* is always [gl]: **glisser** [glise], **église** [egli:z(ə)].

● H

The letter *h* is always silent in French. It may be sounded in foreign words such as "Nahandove" [nahando:və] from Ravel's *Chansons Madécasses*. It is true that French singers sometimes pronounce *h* in situations of strong emotional content (**haine, honte**), but this practice is not advisable for non-French singers until they are very proficient with the language. (For a discussion of aspirate and nonaspirate *h*, see the section "Definition of Terms Relating to French Diction.")

● J

The letter *j* is always pronounced [ʒ]. It is always initial or medial, never final:

juge [ʒy:ʒ (ə)] **jouir** [ʒwi:r] **projet** [prɔʒɛ] **conjoindre** [kõʒwɛ̃:dr(ə)]

● L, LL

When Final

As one of the "careful" consonants, final *l* is usually sounded:

ciel [sjɛl] **idéal** [ideal] **avril** [avril] **seul** [sœl] **nul** [nyl] **cil** [sil]

but words ending in vowel plus *il* end in [j]:

travail [trava:j]	**soleil** [sɔlɛ:j]	**pareil** [parɛ:j]
cercueil [sɛrkœ:j]	**vermeil** [vɛrmɛ:j]	**orgueil** [ɔrgœ:j]
oeil [œ:j]	**deuil** [dœ:j]	

A few words ending in consonant plus *il* have silent *l*:

gentil [ʒɑ̃ti] **fusil** [fyzi] **sourcil** [sursi]

Initial/Medial

As in Italian, [l] must be pronounced forward, with the front of the tongue near or at the upper front teeth:

livre [li:vr(ə)] **galant** [galɑ̃] **fidèle** [fidɛl(ə)]

The word **fils** [fis] meaning *son* or *sons* has silent *l*. The word **fil** [fil] means *thread*; its plural is **fils**, also pronounced [fil].

Double *ll* also sounds as [l]:

aller [ale]   **belle** [bɛl(ə)]   **follement** [fɔl(ə)mã]

although usually *-ill* is [j] or [i:j]:

fille [fi:j(ə)]   **vieillard** [vjɛja:r]   **ailleurs** [ajœ:r]

Exceptions:

mille [mil(ə)],   **tranquille** [trãkil(ə)],   **ville** [vil(ə)]

-ilh- is also [j]:

Milhaud [mijo]   **Anouilh** [anu:j]   **Paladilhe** [paladi:j(ə)]

and initial *ill-* has [ll] (lengthened sound):
illusion [illyzjõ], **illuminer** [illymine].
The combinations *-ault* and *-auld* sound as [o]:

Foucault [fuko]   **Clérambault** [klerãbo]   **Rochefoucauld** [rɔʃ(ə)fuko].

● **M, MM**

When Final

Final *m*, or *m* before final silent consonants, results in a nasal vowel and is therefore silent:

daim [dɛ̃]   **parfum** [parfœ̃]   **thym** [tɛ̃]   **temps** [tã]

Words of foreign origin will sound final *m*: **Jérusalem** [ʒeryzalɛm].

Initial/Medial

If *m* precedes a vowel, it does not cause a nasal vowel, and is therefore [m]:

aime [ɛm(ə)]   **camembert** [kamãbɛ:r]   **maman** [mamã]

m is silent before *n*: **damner** [dɑne], **automne** [otɔn(ə)], with the exception of **hymne** [imn(ə)], **calomnie** [kalɔmni] (and derivatives).

Double *mm* normally sounds as [m]:
femme [fam(ə)], **commencer** [kɔmãse].

Remember that words with initial *emm-* and *remm-* have [ãm]:

emmener [ãm(ə)ne]   **emmêler** [ãmɛle]   **remmener** [rãm(ə)ne]

And initial *imm-* has [mm]:
immense [immãs(ə)], **immortel** [immɔrtɛl].

● N, NN

When Final

Final *n*, or *n* before final silent consonants, results in a nasal vowel and is therefore silent:

soudain [sudɛ̃]	**jambon** [ʒãbõ]	**artisan** [artizã]
dans [dã]	**dent** [dã]	**charmant** [ʃarmã]

Words of foreign origin will sound final *n*: **Carmen** [karmɛn].

Initial/Medial

When *n* precedes a vowel, it does not cause a nasal vowel and is therefore [n]:

soudaine [sudɛn(ə)]   **inutile** [inytil(ə)]   **neige** [nɛ:ʒ(ə)]

Exceptions: a few words with initial *-en* have [ãn]:

enivrer [ãnivre],   **enamourer** [ãnamure],   **enorgueiller** [ãnɔrgœje].

Double *nn* is usually [n]: **mienne** [mjɛn(ə)], **sonner** [sɔne], but initial *inn-* has [nn] (lengthened sound):
innombrable [innõbrabl(ə)], **innocent** [innɔsã].

● P, PP

When Final

Final *p* is normally silent:

trop [tro]   **beaucoup** [boku]   **champ** [ʃã]

but is sounded in a few words: cap [kap].

Initial/Medial

p and *pp* usually sound as [p]:

porte [pɔrt(ə)] **après** [aprɛ] **approcher** [aprɔʃe]

including initial *ps*:

psaume [psom(ə)] **Psyché** [psiʃe] **psychologie** [psikɔlɔʒi]

> *p* before *t* is often silent:

sept [sɛt]	**compter** [kõte]	**baptême** [batɛm(ə)]
prompt [prõ]	**prompte** [prõt(ə)]	**sculpture** [skylty:r(ə)]

but is sounded in some words:

septembre [sɛptã:br(ə)] **crypte** [cript(ə)] **somptueux** [sõptyø]
rédempteur [redãptœ:r]

(Always check a reliable dictionary for the combination *pt*.)
    The combination *ph* sounds as [f]:
philosophe [filɔzɔf(ə)], **philtre** [filtr(ə)].

● Q

The letter *q* sounds as [k] wherever it falls in the word:

quelque [kɛlk(ə)] **coq** [kɔk] **coquin** [kɔkɛ̃] **querelle** [kərɛl(ə)]

The word **cinq** sounds the *q* when standing alone or when followed
by a word beginning with a vowel or *h*. The *q* is silent when **cinq**
is followed by a word beginning with a consonant:

cinq [sɛ̃:k]	**cinq ans** [sɛ̃:k ã]
cinq hommes [sɛ̃:kɔm(ə)]	**cinq femmes** [sɛ̃ fam(ə)]

● R, RR

In singing French art song and opera, *r* has traditionally been pronounced as a flip of the tongue: [r]. In speech and popular singing
the uvular sound [ʀ] is used. Judicious use of the uvular sound, however, has recently become accepted in some circles for "classical"
singing. It is advisable for singers with moderate experience with
French to use the flipped [r] sound. The uvular sound may be considered at some future point if stylistic trends call for it, but only
if recommended by experts in French vocal music.

Double *rr* is lengthened (tongue roll) only in initial *irr-*: **irrésolu** [irrezɔly], **irréel** [irreɛl]. Double *rr* in other contexts normally sounds as [r] (one flip of the tongue):

erreur [ɛrœr]   **horreur** [ɔrœ:r]   **arranger** [arɑ̃ʒe]

although a rolled *rr* is not inappropriate in moments of high intensity.

When Final

As one of the "careful" consonants, the letter *r* is often sounded at the end of a word, but there are frequent and common exceptions.

• Final *r* is sounded in all monosyllables:

mer [mɛ:r]	**pour** [pu:r]	**cher** [ʃɛ:r]	**air** [ɛ:r]
sur [sy:r]	**par** [pa:r]	**ver** [vɛ:r]	**hier** [jɛ:r]
voir [vwa:r]	**fuir** [fɥi:r]	**coeur** [kœ:r]	**fleur** [flœ:r]

• Final *r* is sounded in many nouns and adjectives of two syllables:

amer [amɛ:r]	**amour** [amu:r]	**enfer** [ɑ̃fɛ:r]
hiver [ivɛ:r]	**miroir** [mirwa:r]	**espoir** [ɛspwa:r]

• Final *r* is sounded in many proper names:

Auber [obɛ:r]   **Honegger** [ɔnɛgɛ:r]   **Jupiter** [ʒypitɛ:r]

• Final *r* is sounded in all verb infinitives in *-ir*:

mourir [muri:r]   **venir** [vəni:r]   **découvrir** [dekuvri:r]

• Final *r* is silent in polysyllabic words ending in *-ier*, *-yer*, and *-iller* ([je]):

premier [prəmje]	**dernier** [dɛrnje]	**cahier** [kaje]
métier [metje]	**foyer** [fwaje]	**loyer** [lwaje]
oreiller [ɔrɛje]		

• Final *r* is silent in nouns and adjectives ending *-ser*, *-cher*, and *-ger*:

baiser [beze]	**clocher** [klɔʃe]	**rocher** [rɔʃe]
archer [arʃe]	**léger** [leʒe]	**boucher** [buʃe]
berger [bɛrʒe]	**boulanger** [bulɑ̃ʒe]	**Roger** [rɔʒe]

• Final *r* is silent in all verb infinitives in *-er*:

aller [ale]   **parler** [parle]   **aimer** [eme]
chercher [ʃɛrʃe]   **trouver** [truve]

Initial/Medial

r is always sounded in these positions, including before final silent consonants:

mettre [mɛtr(ə)]   **boucherie** [buʃ(ə)ri]
bergère [bɛrgɛr(ə)]   **première** [prəmjɛr(ə)]
dernière [dɛrnjɛr(ə)]   **tort** [tɔ:r]
vers [vɛ:r]   **regard** [rəga:r]
accord [akɔ:r]

Exception: **gars** [gɑ].

● S, SC, SS

When Final

Final *s* is usually silent:

bas [bɑ]   **pas** [pɑ]   **suis** [sɥi]   **sous** [su]
gens [ʒɑ̃]   **sans** [sɑ̃]   **vous** [vu]   **alors** [alɔ:r]
gars [gɑ]   **corps** [kɔ:r]   **temps** [tɑ̃]

including final *s* indicating plurality of all regular nouns and adjectives: **belles filles** [bɛl(ə) fi:j(ə)], **les haricots verts** [lɛ ariko vɛ:r], and final *s* in all verb forms:
tu aimes [ty ɛm(ə)], **nous aimons** [nuzɛmõ].

Final *s* is sounded as [s] in a number of words:

fils [fis]   **lys** (also lis) [lis]   **ours** [urs]
hélas [elɑs]   **angélus** [ɑ̃ʒelys]   **jadis** [ʒadis]
iris [iris]   **sus** [sys]   **prospectus** [prɔspɛktys]

The word **os** in the singular is [ɔs]. The plural is **os**, pronounced [o].
The word **sens** as a noun (*sense*) is [sɑ̃:s]. As a verb (from **sentir**) it is [sɑ̃].
When the word **tous** modifies a noun, it is [tu]: **tous les deux** [tu lɛ dø]. When it is a pronoun (not modifying a noun) it is [tus]: **entre tous** [ɑ̃:tr(ə)tus].
Final *s* is sounded in many proper names:

Francis [frɑ̃sis]   **Thaïs** [tais]   **Saint-Saëns** [sɛ̃ sɑ̃:s]
Damis [damis]   **Tircis** [tirsis]   **Vénus** [venys]
Mars [mars]   **Atlas** [atlas]   **Cérès** [serɛs]
Baucis [bosis]   **Reims** [rɛ̃:s]

though it is silent in others:

Charles [ʃarl(ə)]   **Chartres** [ʃartr(ə)]   **Thomas** [tɔma]

Initial/Medial

As in other languages, *s* has two sounds: unvoiced [s] and voiced [z]. Unvoiced *s* occurs initially before a vowel: **soir** [swar], **silence** [silɑ̃:s(ə)]. It occurs initially or medially before or after an unvoiced consonant:

aspect [aspɛ]   **structure** [strykty:r(ə)]   **tocsin** [tɔksɛ̃]

Unvoiced *s* occurs medially after nasal vowels: **danser** [dɑ̃se].
   Although the prefix *trans-* has [z] when followed by a vowel or *h*:

transir [trɑ̃zi:r]   **transhumer** [trɑ̃zyme]   **transitif** [trɑ̃zitif]

it has [s] when followed by a consonant or mute *e*:

transmettre [trɑ̃smetr(ə)]   **transborder** [trɑ̃sborde]   **transe** [trɑ̃s(ə)]

   In the combinations *sce* and *sci*, the c assimilates with the *s* to sound as [s]:

descendre [desɑ̃dr(ə)]   **piscine** [pisin]   **science** [sjɑ̃:s(ə)]

Double *ss* is [s]:

classe [klɑ:s(ə)]   **laisser** [lɛse] or [lese]   **poisson** [pwasõ]

In contrast to Italian, *s* preceding a voiced consonant is unvoiced:

svelte [svɛlt(ə)]   **jasmin** [ʒasmɛ̃]   **transmettre** [trɑ̃smɛtr(ə)]
transborder [trɑ̃sbɔrde]

Voiced *s* occurs between vowel-letters:

rose [ro:z(ə)]   **croiser** [krwɑze]   **hasard** [aza:r]

and in liaison (see "Liaison"): **mes amis** [mɛzami].

When *s* appears intervocalic, but begins the second part of a compound word, it is unvoiced: **susurrer** [sysyre].

● T, TT, TH

When Final

Final *t* is usually silent:

mot [mo]	**chat** [ʃa]	**doigt** [dwa]	**vient** [vjɛ̃]
petit [p(ə)ti]	**effet** [efɛ]	**effort** [efɔ:r]	**aspect** [aspɛ]
argent [arʒɑ̃]	**Albert** [albɛ:r]	**Hamlet** [amlɛ]	

but it is sounded in a few words:

dot [dɔt]	**est** (meaning east) [ɛst]	**ouest** [wɛst]
huit [ɥit]	**brut** [bryt]	**direct** [dirɛkt]
exact [egzakt]	**Ernest** [ɛrnɛst]	**Tybalt** [tibalt]

The word **soit** when standing alone as an interjection sounds the *t*:
Soit! [swat]; otherwise the *t* is silent:

Honi soit qui mal y pense [ɔni swa ki mal i pɑ̃:s(ə)].

The word **Christ** is [krist], but **Jésus-Christ** is [ʒesy kri].

Initial/Medial

The sound [t] is to be pronounced with no aspiration. The front of
the tongue must contact the back of the upper front teeth. It is the
same sound as in Italian:

tête [tɛt(ə)]   **artiste** [artist(ə)]   **petite** [p(ə)tit(ə)]

Double *tt* and *th* also sound as [t]:

étiquette [etikɛt(ə)]   **attendre** [atɑ̃:dr(ə)]   **théâtre** [teɑtr(ə)]   **thé** [te]

In the suffixes *-tion*, *-tience*, *-tien(ne)*, *-tient(e)*, *-tiel(le)*, *-tieux(se)*,
and *-tiable*, (after a vowel) the *ti* sounds as [sj]:

nation [nasjõ]	**déploration** [deplɔrasjõ]
patience [pasjɑ̃:s(ə)]	**patient** [pasjɑ̃]
patiente [pasjɑ̃:t(ə)]	**vénitien** [venisjɛ̃]
vénitienne [venisjɛn(ə)]	**essentiel** [ɛsɑ̃sjɛl]
torrentiel [tɔrɑ̃sjɛl]	**minutieux** [minysjø]
insatiable [ɛ̃sasjabl(ə)]	

Final *-tie* sounds as [si]: **Helvétie** [ɛlvesi]. (Notice the similar-
ity to English, which has [ʃ] or [tʃ] in these words.)
But other suffixes with *ti* have [tj], including sometimes *-tien(ne)*

chrétien [kretjɛ̃]   **antienne** [ɑ̃tjɛn(ə)]   **entretien** [ɑ̃trətjɛ̃]
sentier [sɑ̃tje]   **cimetière** [simitjɛ:r(ə)]

And *-tion* following *s* is [tj]: **question** [kɛstjõ], **digestion**
[diʒɛstjõ].

● V

The letter *v* is found only in initial and medial positions and is always [v]. It is never doubled.

venir [vəniːr]   **vingt** [vɛ̃]   **vieux** [vjø]   **avoir** [avwaːr]   **naïveté** [naiv(ə)te]

● W

w is essentially a foreign letter to French and is therefore found in foreign words, in initial positions only. Words from German use [v] and words from English use [w], though some English-derived words use [v]:

wagon [vagõ]   **whiskey** [wiski]   **Watteau** [vato]

● X

When Final

The letter *x* is usually silent when final:

deux [dø]   **voix** [vwa]   **faux** [fo], but **Aix** [ɛks]

When standing alone, the numbers **six** and **dix** sound the *x* as [s]. Final *x* sounds as [ks] in a few words:

index [ɛ̃dɛks]	**sphinx** [sfɛ̃ːks]	**syrinx** [sirɛ̃ːks]
lynx [lɛ̃ːks]	**Béatrix** [beatriks]	**Cadix** [kadiks]

Initial/Medial

As in English, initial *x* is rare. It usually sounds as [ks]: **xylophone** [ksilɔfɔn]. Sometimes it sounds as [gz]: **Xavier** [gzavje].
    Medial *x* is usually [ks]:

fixer [fikse]   **extrême** [ɛkstrɛm(ə)]   **mixte** [mikst(ə)]

The proper name **Bruxelles** is [brysɛl].

Initial *ex* followed by a vowel or *h* is [ɛgz]:

exemple [ɛgzã:pl(ə)]   **exercice** [ɛgzɛrsis(ə)]   **exhaler** [ɛgzale]
exhiber [ɛgzibe]

In numerical words, *-xième* has [z]:

deuxième [døzjɛm(ə)] **sixième** [sizjɛm(ə)] **dixième** [dizjɛm(ə)]
and **soixante** has [s]: [swasɑ̃t(ə)]

In liaison, *x* sounds as [z]: **deux amis** [dø zami] (see "Liaison").

● **Z**

When Final

Final *z* is usually silent, including all second person plural verb
forms:

chez [ʃe] **nez** [ne] **dormez** [dɔrme] **partirez** [partire]

It is sounded as [z] in several proper names:
Berlioz [bɛrljoːz], **Boulez** [bulɛːz].

Initial/Medial

In any position other than final, *z* sounds as [z]:

zéro [zero] **zèle** [zɛl(ə)] **seize** [sɛːz(ə)] **treize** [trɛːz(ə)] **azur** [azyːr]

Liaison

Liaison is the sounding of an otherwise silent final consonant when
the following word begins with a vowel or unaspirated *h*. Not every
final consonant preceding a vowel is sounded, however, but it occurs
more often in singing than in speech. (*Note:* Long vowels are indicated in IPA only when final in a phrase.)

When liaison occurs, some letters change their sounds:

- *d* sounds as [t]:
  quand il pleut [kɑ̃ til plø], **grand arbre** [grɑ̃ tarbr(ə)].
- *g* sounds as [k]:
  long hiver [lɔ̃ kivɛːr], **sang impur** [sɑ̃ kɛ̃pyːr].

These two letters are rarely in liaison, however. The letter *f* is normally sounded when final, so it technically does not cause liaison,
but when **neuf** is followed by **heures** or **ans**, it changes its sound
to [v]: **neuf ans** [nœ vɑ̃].

- *s* sounds as [z], as it does intervocalically: **tes yeux** [tɛ zjø].

- *x* also sounds as [z]:
  six heures [si zœ:r(ə)], **je veux aller** [jə vø zale].

The remaining consonant-letters that can sound in liaison are *n, r, t*, and *z*. They keep their normal sounds.

When nasal vowels are involved in liaison by sounding *n*, sometimes nasality is eliminated (note that *m* is never in liaison). This varies with different speakers, but common examples are:

- **bon** loses nasality and the vowel is opened:
  bon anniversaire [bɔ naniverse:r(ə)].
- The endings *-ain* and *-ein* lose nasality:
  vain espoir [vɛ nɛspwa:r], **plein air** [plɛ nɛ:r].
- The three adjectives **ancien**, **divin**, and **moyen** lose nasality: **ancien ami** [ɑ̃sjɛ nami], **divin enfant** [divi nɑ̃fɑ̃], **moyen age** [mwajɛ na:ʒ(ə)].

A very few nonnasal vowels change quality in liaison:

- The adverb **trop** has an open vowel in liaison:
  trop heureux [trɔ pørø].
- Adjectives with final *-er* open the vowel in liaison:
  premier amour [prəmjɛ ramu:r], **léger appétit** [leʒɛ rap(ə)ti].
- Verb infinitives in liaison, however, retain closed [e]:
  aimer et loisir [eme re lwazi:r].

Notice that the sound of the above adjectives in liaison is the same as the feminine form of the word (e.g., **bonne, ancienne, divine, moyenne, première, légère**).

In general, liaison occurs between words that are grammatically closely related. Such situations are said to have obligatory liaison. Exceptions occur in specific situations.

- Articles: **un arbre** [œ̃narbr(ə)], **les oiseaux** [lɛzwazo]
- Adjectives: **petit enfant** [pətitɑ̃fɑ̃], **mon amour** [mõnamu:r], **deux hommes** [døzɔm(ə)]
- Pronouns:
  ils ont [ilzõ], **vous êtes** [vuzɛt(ə)], **nous avons** [nuzavõ]
- Verbs: **elle est aimable** [ɛl ɛ tɛmabl(ə)], **ils sont arrivés** [il sõ tarive], **aimer et loisir** [eme re lwazir], **dirent alors** [dirə talɔ:r], including all hyphenated, inverted forms: **vont-ils?** [võ til]
- Adverbs: **trop ouvert** [trɔ puvɛ:r], **bien écri** [bjɛ̃ nekri], **tout heureux** [tu tørø]
- Prepositions: **dans un bois** [dɑ̃ zœ̃ bwa], **en hiver** [ɑ̃ nivɛ:r], **sans amour** [sɑ̃ zamu:r]

- Conjunctions: **quant à** [kɑ̃ ta], **mais avant** [mɛ zavɑ̃], **quand il pleut** [kɑ̃ til plø] (Exception: never liaison after **et**: **lui et elle** [lɥi e ɛl(ə)] but before **et** is fine: **droits et majestueux** [drwɑ ze maʒɛstɥø].)
- Nouns in the plural: **les États-Unis** [le zeta zyni] **désirs inapaisés** [dezir zinapeze]
- But generally *not* nouns in the singular:

  le printemps est venu [lə prɛ̃tɑ̃ ɛ vəny]
  la nuit immense [la nɥi immɑ̃:s(ə)]
  de paix et de douceur [də pɛ e də dusœ:r]
  au pays où se fait la guerre [o pei u sə fɛ la gɛr(ə)]
  le vent a changé [lə vɑ̃ a ʃɑ̃ʒe]

Some common/traditional phrases may have liaison after singular nouns in singing:

  Bois épais [bwa zepɛ]
  quand leur voix appelle [kɑ̃ lœr vwa zapɛl(ə)]
  cet enfant a dormi [sɛt ɑ̃fɑ̃ ta dɔrmi]
  nuit et jour [nɥi te ʒu:r]
  de temps en temps [də tɑ̃ zɑ̃ tɑ̃]

A few exceptions (situations where liaison may not occur) to the above patterns have been noted. Other situations where liaison may not occur are listed below, starting with those already mentioned. These are said to have "forbidden liaison":

- After nouns in the singular: *as above*
- After the word **et**: *as above*
- After a proper noun: **Paris est beau** [pari ɛ bo]
- *Before* the word **oui**: **il a dit oui** [il a di wi]
- Before the numbers **huit** and **onze**: **les huit** [lɛ ɥit]   **les onze** [lɛ ɔ̃:z(ə)] except compound numbers with **huit**: **dix-huit** [dizɥit]
- Usually before or after the word **un** as a number or pronoun:

  j'en vois un [ʒɑ̃ vwa œ̃]
  un ou deux [œ̃ u dø]
  plus d'un aurait donné sa vie [ply dœ̃ ɔrɛ dɔne sa vi(ə)]

  This includes **chacun** and **quelqu'un** and also the plural pronoun **eux**: **chacun à son goût** [ʃakœ̃ a sɔ̃ gu]
  But **un** as an article takes liaison:
  sont un passe-temps [sɔ̃ tœ̃ pa:s(ə) tɑ̃], **un autre** [œ̃ no:tr(ə)]
- Before an aspirate *h*:
  les héros [le ero], **des haies** [dɛ ɛ], **les hauts talons** [lɛ o talɔ̃]

- More generally, when there is a natural lift or break in the phrase between the two words. Sometimes this is indicated by punctuation, although orthographic punctuation does not always forbid liaison.

  les houles, en roulant . . . [lɛ ul(ə) ɑ̃ rulɑ̃]
  en partant, au baiser d'adieu [ɑ̃ partɑ̃ o beze dadjø]
  Vois, il souffle juste assez d'air [vwa il suflə ʒyst ase dɛːr]

- Words that end in *-rd*, *-rs*, and *-rt* normally pronounce the *r* while the final consonant-letter is silent: **hasard** [azaːr], **vers** [vɛːr], **mort** [mɔːr]. Liaison is therefore not called for because the r is already sounded:

  son regard est doux [sɔ̃ rəgaːr ɛ du]
  me penchant vers elle [mə pɑ̃ʃɑ̃ vɛr ɛl(ə)]
  dort un clair de lune [dɔr œ̃ klɛr də lyn(ə)]
  tout couvert encore [tu kuvɛːr ɑ̃kɔːrə]

  Exceptions occur with final *-rs* when the *s* indicates plurality:

  si mes vers avaient des ailes [si mɛ vɛr zavɛ dɛ zɛl(ə)]
  leurs yeux [lœr zjø]
  chers instants [ʃɛr zɛ̃stɑ̃]

  Also the word **toujours** may have the *s* in liaison if it modifies the next word or is modified by it:
  toujours heureux [tuʒur zørø].
- Between two words that are not closely related grammatically. This is often the case with words before or after a prepositional phrase or clause:

  Chanson Triste (Duparc)
  pour mon esprit ont les charmes [pur mɔ̃ nɛspri ɔ̃ lɛʃarm(ə)]
  (No liaison into **ont** because its subject, **soleils**, occurs before the prepositional phrase **pour mon esprit**, which does not refer to **ont**.)

  Lydia (Fauré)
  le jour qui luit est le meilleur [lə ʒur ki lɥi ɛ lə mɛjœːr]
  (No liaison into **est** because its subject is **jour**, modified by **qui luit**.)

  Après un Rêve (Fauré)
  les cieux pour nous entr'ouvraient leurs nues [lɛ sjø puːr nu ɑ̃truvrɛ lœːr nyə]
  (No liaison into **entr'ouvraient** because its subject is **cieux**.)

Adieu (Fauré)
Et je dis en quittant vos charmes [e jə di ɑ̃ kitɑ̃ vo ʃarm(ə)]
(The object of the verb **dis** comes later; it is not **en quittant**.)

- For reasons of euphony:

tant de baisers et de tendresse [tɑ̃ də beze e də tɑ̃drɛs(ə)]
(No laison to avoid consecutive syllables of [zeze].)

- To avoid lack of textual clarity:

dont le chant invite à clore les yeux [dõ lə ʃɑ̃ ɛ̃vit a klɔːr(ə) lɛ zjø]
(No liaison to avoid possible confusion with **t'invite**.)

● Optional Liaison

Prepositional phrases often result in situations of so-called "optional liaision," in which it is the singer's choice whether to execute liaision or not. If the prepositional phrase or clause does relate to an adjacent word, liaison may occur, but it is not always required:

ces cris au loin [sɛ kri zo lwɛ̃] or [sɛ kri o lwɛ̃]
et monter à mes yeux [e mõte ra mɛ zjø] or [e mõte a mɛ zjø]
demandez à la mer [dəmɑ̃de za la mɛːr] or [dəmɑ̃de a la mɛːr]
Fleurit avec la marjolaine [flœri tavɛk la marʒɔlɛn(ə)] or [flœri avɛk]
la route qu'il poursuit en dansant [pursɥi tɑ̃] or [pursɥi ɑ̃]

However many situations with prepositional phrases clearly call for liaison:

tout en chantant [tu tɑ̃ ʃɑ̃tɑ̃]
devant vous à genoux [dəvɑ̃ vu za ʒənu]

Liaison is a complex matter, and confusing to the beginner. Pierre Bernac's book *The Interpretation of French Song* is an excellent resource for many reasons, but particularly because his annotations of song texts indicate when liaison should occur. Unfortunately he does not explain his choices in cases of optional laision, and many songs are not in the book. Careful study of his examples, however, will lead the student to a clearer understanding of this phenomenon.

Musical Settings of Mute e [ə]

When a syllable with mute *e* is given its own pitch by a composer, and elision (see below) does not apply, the [ə] is sung and is equivalent to the vowel sound [œ]. This is the most common way in which vocal music treats mute *e*:

Manon

É - pou - se quel - que bra - ve fil - le
[epuːzə kɛlkə braːvə fiːjə]

Nuit d'Étoiles (Debussy)

Nuit d'é - toi - les   Sous- tes voi - les
[nɥi detwalə su tɛ vwalə]

When a mute *e* ends a word and the next word begins with a vowel, the mute *e* is usually not pronounced. This is "elision" as defined on p. 119.

Voici que le printemps (Debussy)

flot - te u - ne om - bre   va - gue et ten - dre
[flɔt yn õːbrə vag e tãːdrə]

Recueillement (Debussy)

U - ne at - mos - phè - re ob - scu - re en - ve - lop - pe la   vil - le
[yn atmɔsfɛːr ɔpskyːr ãvələpə la vilə]

In the following example note the slur, indicating that the syllable [lõ] is to be sung on both the A and G, with elision causing [ʒy] to be sung on the F sharp. It is wrong to sing schwa on the G, as at least one edition of this song implies:

pro - lon - ge u - ne chan - son
[prɔlõːʒ ynə ʃãsõ]

*Voici que le
printemps (Debussy)*

When mute *e* follows a vowel, it is, as usual, silent in speech:

soie [swa]   **joie** [ʒwa]   **joue** [ʒu]   **queue** [kø]
gaiement [gemɑ̃] **gaieté** [gete]   **vie** [vi]   **amie** [ami]
rue [ry]   **vues** [vy]

When mute *e* follows a vowel and is final in the word, it will usually be set musically as schwa:

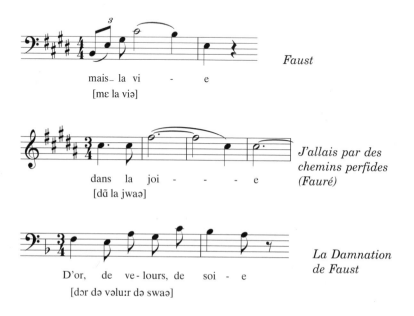

Faust

mais la vi - e
[mɛ la viə]

*J'allais par des
chemins perfides
(Fauré)*

dans la joi - - e
[dɑ̃ la jwaə]

*La Damnation
de Faust*

D'or, de ve - lours, de soi - e
[dɔr də vəlu:r də swaə]

Sometimes such words will be set without schwa:

Réponse d'une épouse sage (Roussel)

froi- de - ment sur la soie de ma ro - be
[frwadəmɑ̃ syr la swa də ma rɔbə]

La flûte enchantée (Ravel)

Vers ma joue comme un my - sté - ri - eux bai - ser
[vɛr ma ʒu kɔ mœ̃misterjø beze]

When mute *e* is medial after a vowel it is always silent, even in singing:

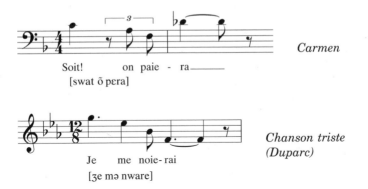

Soit!   on paie - ra⎯⎯⎯   *Carmen*
[swat ɔ̃ pɛra]

Je   me noie- rai   *Chanson triste*
[ʒe mə nware]   *(Duparc)*

A common pattern involving schwa is the feminine ending *-ée(s)*. The most usual type of musical setting separates it into two sounds: [eə]. The singer must be careful that no intervening [j] sound occurs when moving from one sound to the next. This is of course true in any instance of a vowel sound preceding schwa, but it seems to be a particular problem with this combination.

L'Absence (Berlioz)

Re- viens, re - viens,⎯   ma bien - ai - mé - e
[rəvjɛ̃ rəvjɛ̃ ma bjɛ̃nemeə]

La lune blanche (Fauré)

sous la   ra - mé - - - e⎯
[su la rameə]

De grève (Debussy)

Soie verte i - ri - sé - e
[swa vɛrt irizeə]

Occasionally this pattern will be set as [e] only:

Pelléas et Mélisande

el - les se sont ré - fu - giées du cô - té de
[εlə sə sõ refyʒje dy kote də]

l'om - bre
[lõ:brə]

Le paon (Ravel)

du reste— de la jour - née
[dy rɛst(ə) də la ʒurne]

De soir (Debussy)

Où mes pen - sées tris - te
[u mɛ pãse tristə]

When a composer sets a mute *e* as the second of a pair of tied notes, and elision does not apply, there are various possibilities of execution:

1. If the tied note value is of short duration and the mute *e* is preceded by a consonant, the note is used to articulate the consonant with a brief (often very brief) [ə] sound following.

La caravane (Chausson)

La——— su - eur——— qui— l'i - nonde——
[la syœr ki linõ:d(ə)]

L'Ombre des arbres (Debussy)

Se plaign - ent   les tour - te - relles——
[sə plɛɲə lɛ turtərɛl(ə)]

Carmen

que rien ne m'é - pou - van - te
[kə rjɛ̃ nə mepuvɑ̃t(ə)]

2. If the tied note value is sufficiently long the [ə] may be more sustained (as [œ]).

Green (Debussy)

de   la   bon - ne   tem - pê - te
[də la bɔnə tɑ̃pɛtə]

Cantique à l'épouse (Chausson)

Nuit   fré - mis - san - te,   mys - ti - (que)
[nɥi fremisɑ̃:tə mistikə]

3. If the mute *e*, preceded by a vowel, is not separated syllabically in the text underlay, it is silent.

de   la   pluie!——
[də la plɥi]

Il pleure dans mon coeur (Debussy)

J'al - lais ê - tre   la proie——
[ʒalɛ zɛ:trə la prwa]

Carmen

4. If it is separated syllabically, the tied note will sound as schwa.

Il pleure dans mon coeur (Debussy)

qui s'en - nui - e
[ki sɑ̃ɥiə]

In settings by twentieth-century composers, particularly Ravel, mute *e* is often not pronounced. There is either no note for the schwa, or a tied note of short duration that suggests the articulation of the following consonant with little or no vowel sound after it.

Le martin-pêcheur (Ravel)

Com- me je te - nais ma per - che de ligne ten - due
[kɔm(ə) ʒə tənɛ ma pɛrʃ(ə) də liɲ(ə) tɑ̃dy]

Placet futile (Debussy)

ni du rouge, ni jeux miè - vres
[ni dy ruːʒ(ə) ni ʒø mjɛːvr(ə)]

This can even lead in some instances to complete elision of mute *e*'s as in speech:

Le cygne (Ravel)

mais q'est-ce que je dis?
[mɛ kɛs kə ʒ di]

Compare these two settings of the word **paysage**:

Le son du cor (Debussy)

un pa - y - sa - ge lent
[œ̃ peizaːʒə lɑ̃]

Shéhérazade (Ravel)

à loi - sir des pa - y - sa - ges peints
[a lwa ziːr de pe(i)zaːʒ(ə) pɛ̃]

The first clearly sets four syllables, while the second suggests two.

Remember that some forms of the verb **faire** pronounce *ai* as schwa:

Shéhérazade (Ravel)

Me **fai**- sant un der- nier geste a - vec grâ - ce
[mə fəzɑ̃ tœ̃ dɛrnje ʒɛst avɛk grɑːs(ə)]

Carmen

De leurs in - struments fai- saient ra - ge
[də lœr zɛ̃strymɑ̃ fəzɛ raːʒə]

Musical Settings of Glides

● **[j]**

In patterns of *i* plus vowel, musical settings often treat [j] as [i]:

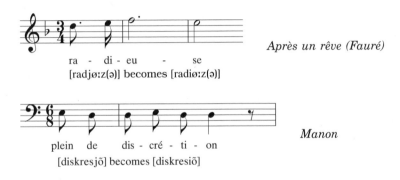

ra - di - eu - se
[radjøːz(ə)] becomes [radiøːz(ə)]

Après un rêve (Fauré)

plein de dis - cré - ti - on
[diskresjɔ̃] becomes [diskresiɔ̃]

Manon

although similar situations sometimes find the musical setting keeping the glide:

Jazz dans la nuit (Roussel)

ir - ra - diés——
[irradje]

Pelléas et Mélisande

et   ce ma-riage   al - lait met - tre   fin
[et sə marja:ʒ alə mɛtrə fɛ̃]

Le paon (Ravel)

C'est ain - si qu'il ap- pelle sa fian- cée
[sɛ tɛ̃si kil apɛl sa fjãse]

    Remember that *i* followed by mute *e* medially in a word is just [i]. There is no glide.

Faust

Tu   re - nie - ras, pour vi - vre
[ty rənira pur vi:vrə]

● **[w]**

When [w] is spelled *ou*, composers usually set it as the vowel [u]:

La Damnation de Faust

à ses   pieds——   ma lou - an - ge?
[lwã:ʒə] becomes [luã:ʒə]

La lune blanche
(Fauré)

La sil - hou - et - te
[silwɛt(ə)] becomes [siluɛt(ə)]

although sometimes such words will be set retaining the glide:

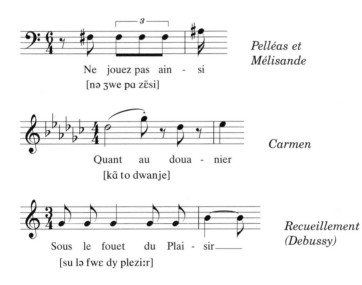

Pelléas et
Mélisande

Ne jouez pas ain - si
[nə ʒwe pɑ zɛ̃si]

Carmen

Quant au doua - nier
[kɑ̃ to dwanje]

Recueillement
(Debussy)

Sous le fouet du Plai - sir
[su lə fwɛ dy plezi:r]

● [ɥ]

When *ui* follows a single consonant, such as **lui**, **fui**, **nuit**, **suivi**, **puissance**, musical settings retain the glide-vowel pattern. The [ɥi] combination occurs as one syllable on one note.

When *ui* follows a consonant plus *l* or *r*, they divide into two syllables as [yi]:

La Damnation de Faust

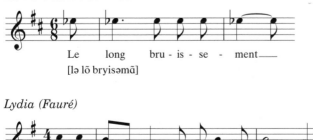

Le long bru - is - se - ment
[lə lõ bryisəmɑ̃]

Lydia (Fauré)

L'or flu - i - de que tu dé - nou - es
[lɔr flyidə kə ty denuə]

When [ɥ] is followed by vowels other than [i], musical settings usually treat [ɥ] as the vowel [y], creating another syllable:

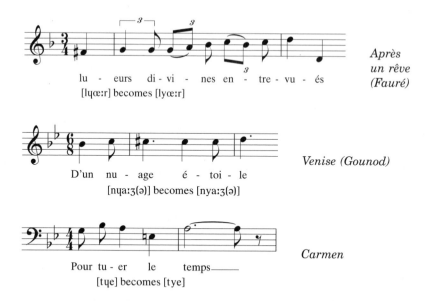

lu - eurs di - vi - nes en - tre - vu - és

[lɥœːr] becomes [lyœːr]

Après un rêve (Fauré)

D'un nu - age é - toi - le

[nɥaːʒ(ə)] becomes [nyaːʒ(ə)]

Venise (Gounod)

Pour tu - er le temps____

[tɥe] becomes [tye]

Carmen

although sometimes such words are set retaining the glide:

ce grand nua - ge

[sə grɑ̃ nɥaːʒ(ə)]

Pelléas et Mélisande

Les vo - lailles ha - bi - tuées ne lèvent

[le vɔlaj(ə) zabitɥe nə lɛvə]

Le paon (Ravel)

Remember that final -*ue* is either [y] or [yə], and medial *ue* (except after *c*, *g*, and *q*) is just [y]:

Elle est per - due... per - du - e!

[ɛl ɛ pɛrdy pɛrdyə]

Pelléas et Mélisande

Je   le   tue - rai!
[ʒə lə tyre]

Faust

Vowel Length

Although vowel length for singing is largely a factor of note values assigned by the composer, understanding vowel length is important to the singer in making subtle differences in articulating vowel-to-consonant relationships. Such understanding is even more important in music that approximates speech patterns, as, for example, much of Debussy's *Pelléas et Mélisande* and much twentieth-century art song repertoire.

There is not absolute unanimity among phoneticians in defining all cases of long vowels in French. All, however, agree on the following:

All French vowels in syllables other than the final are short. Vowels in *final* syllables (excluding mute *e*) *may* be long if one of the following applies:

- Nasal vowels are lengthened when followed by a pronounced consonant:

  dans [dɑ̃] versus **danse**[dɑ̃:s(ə)]
  vin [vɛ̃] versus **timbre** [tɛ̃:br(ə)]
  fond [fõ] versus **fondre** [fõ:dr(ə)]
  défunt [defœ̃] versus **défunte** [defœ̃:t(ə)]

- [ɑ], [o], [ø] are lengthened when followed by a pronounced consonant:

  pas [pɑ] versus **passe** [pɑ:s(ə)]
  chaud [ʃo] versus **chaude** [ʃo:d(ə)]
  jeune [ʒœn(ə)] versus **jeûne** [ʒø:n(ə)] ([ø] plus consonant is rare)

  including all words ending in -euse:
  chanteuse [ʃɑ̃tø:z(ə)],   **heureuse** [ørø:z (ə)].

- Circumflex vowels are lengthened when followed by a pronounced consonant:

  tel [tɛl] versus **tête** [tɛ:t(ə)]
  faites [fɛt(ə)] versus **fêtes** [fɛ:t(ə)]
  il [il] versus **île** [i:l(ə)]   **mettre** [mɛtr(ə)] versus **maître** [mɛ:tr(ə)]

(Exceptions with verb forms: **êtes** [ɛt(ə)])

- *All* vowels are lengthened when followed by [z], [ʒ], [v], [r], or [vr] as the final sound of the word:

douce [dus(ə)] versus **douze** [du:z(ə)]
furtif [fyrtif] versus **furtive** [fyrti:v(ə)]
baisse [bɛs(ə)] versus **beige** [bɛ:ʒ(ə)] versus **reine** [rɛn(ə)]
accort [akɔ:r] versus **accorte** [akɔrt(ə)] versus **accoste** [akɔst(ə)]
libre [libr(ə)] versus **livre** [li:vr(ə)]
régal [regal] versus **regard** [rəga:r]

Some phoneticians consider final [j] or [jə] to lengthen the preceding vowel:

soleil [sɔlɛ:j]   **travail** [trava:j]   **feuille** [fœ:j(ə)]

This text indicates long vowels in the situations listed above, although syntactical shortening of some long vowels may occur within phrases.

Bibliography

Bernac, Pierre. *The Interpretation of French Song*. New York: W.W. Norton & Co., 1970.

Camilli, Amerindo. *An Italian Phonetic Reader*. London: University of London Press, 1921.

———. *Pronuncia e Grafia dell'Italiano*. Florence: Sansoni Editore, 1943.

Carton, Fernand. *Introduction à la Phonétique du Français*. Paris: Bordas, 1974.

Castel, Nico. *The Complete Puccini Librettos*. Geneseo, N.Y.: Leyerle Publications, 1993.

———. *A Singer's Manual of Spanish Lyric Diction*. New York: Excalibur, 1994.

Castiglione, Pierina Borrani. *Italian Phonetics, Diction and Intonation*. New York: S.F. Vanni, 1957.

Colorni, Evelina. *Singer's Italian*. New York: Schirmer Books, 1970.

Cox, Richard G. *The Singer's Manual of German and French Diction*. New York: Schirmer Books, 1970.

Duden Aussprachewörterbuch. Mannheim: Dudenverlag, 1990.

Fouché, Pierre. *Traité de Prononciation Française*. Paris: Librairie C.Klinckrieck, 1957.

Grubb, Thomas. *Singing in French*. New York: Schirmer Books, 1979.

Léon, Pierre R. *Prononciation du Français Standard*. Paris: Didier, 1978.

Malécot, André. *Introduction à la Phonétique Français*. The Hague: Mouton, 1977.

Martinet, André, and Henriette Walter. *Dictionnaire de la Prononciation Française dans son Usage Réel.* Paris: France—Expansion, 1973.

Moriarty, John. *Diction.* Boston: E. C. Schirmer Music Company, 1975.

Nitze, William, et. al. *A Handbook of French Phonetics.* New York: Henry Holt and Co., 1913.

Odom, William. *German for Singers.* New York: Schirmer Books, 1981.

Rothmüller, Marko. *Pronunciation of German and German Diction.* Bloomington, Ind.: Published by author, 1978.

Schane, Sanford. *French Phonology and Morphology.* Cambridge, Mass.: MIT Press, 1968.

Sheil, Richard F. *A Manual of Foreign Language Dictions for Singers.* Arcade, N.Y.: Palladian Co., 1979.

Siebs, Theodor. *Deutsche Aussprache.* Berlin: Walter de Gruyter & Co., 1969.

Stapp, Marci. *The Singer's Guide to Languages.* San Francisco: Published by author, 1991.

Valdman, Albert. *Introduction to French Phonology and Morphology.* Rowley, Mass.: Newbury House Publishers, Inc., 1968.

Wall, Joan, et. al. *Diction.* Dallas: Pst, 1990.

Walter, Henriette. *La Phonologie du Français.* Paris: Presses Universitaires de France, 1977.

GENERAL INDEX

Acute accent: Italian, 3; French, 117
Apocopation , 6–7
Aspirated *h*, 119
Assimilation: of *n*, Italian, 30–31; of consonants, German, 111–14

Breakdown of mixed vowels. *See* Mixed vowels

Cedilla, 118, 144
Circumflex: Italian, 3; French, 118
Closed vowels. *See* Vowel quality
Consonant clusters: Italian, 35–36; German phrasal, 108–11
Consonant length, Italian, 19–20
Consonants: Italian, 19; 21; Italian single and double, 19–20, 32–33; articulating double in singing Italian, 33–34; non-aspiration of Italian, 1, 19, 21; dental pronunciation of Italian, 1, 21; German double, 94; de-voicing of German, 98–99, 102; French, 141–42; French double, 124. *See also* Index of sounds, Phrasal doubling

De-voicing of consonants. *See* Consonants
Diacritical Marks: Italian, 3–4; German, 69; French, 117–18
Dictionaries: Italian, 2–3, German, 68–69; French, 116–17
Dieresis: Italian, 4; French, 118

Diphthongs: Italian, 16–18; musical settings of Italian, 38–40; vowel distribution in singing, Italian, 40–43; phrasal, Italian, 43–44; vowel distribution in singing phrasal, Italian, 44–50; inappropriate, 1, 13–14; German, 92–93; English, 72–73, 75, 76, 93
Double consonants. *See* Consonants

Elision, 119, 161

Flipped *r*: xiii; Italian, 19, 22–23; German, 97; French, 150–51. *See also* index of sounds

Glides: Italian, 14–15; German, 93–94; French, 139–141; musical settings of French, 167–71
Glottal attack, 73, 103–104
Glottal separation in singing German, 104–8
Grave accent: Italian, 3–4; French, 117

International phonetic alphabet (IPA): xii–xiv; Italian, symbols for, 2; German, symbols for, 68; French, symbols for, 116

Liaison, 119, 156–60
Linking of vowels. *See* Diphthongs, Italian phrasal

175

INDEX OF SOUNDS
BY SPELLING